THE BAT
ONE YOUNG AMERICAN

By
David Vining

https://davidmvining.wordpress.com/

© 2018 David Vining

ISBN: 9781718004528

Battle of Lake Erie, 10 September 1813 by C.R. Patterson & H.B. French

To Mom and Dad.

Contents

CHAPTER 1: Morning..1

CHAPTER II: Tales Told at Sea 13

CHAPTER III: At the Commodore's Table 21

CHAPTER IV: March Over Water...36

CHAPTER V: The Battle Begins 49

CHAPTER VI: Tactical Retreat...63

CHAPTER VII: Headfirst..72

CHAPTER VIII: Evening 79

Bibliography 97

List of Illustrations

Battle of Lake Erie, 10 September 1813 by C.R. Patterson & H.B. French.................................iii

Partie Occidentale de la Nouvelle France ou du Canada by Jacques Nicolas Bellin..............1

Bataille des Saintes by Thomas Whitcombe 13

Portrait of Oliver Hazard Perry by Gilbert Stuart..21

The Brig Niagara by Lance Woodworth 36

"12 Noon" from The Naval War of 1812 by Theodore Roosevelt...............................49

"2 P.M." from The Naval War of 1812 by Theodore Roosevelt.....................................63

"2:50 P.M." from The Naval War of 1812 by Theodore Roosevelt 72

Perry's Victory on Lake Erie by Thomas Birch 79

CHAPTER 1: Morning

Partie Occidentale de la Nouvelle France ou du Canada by Jacques Nicolas Bellin

Ding ding. Ding ding. Ding ding. Ding.

"One, two, three, four, five, six, seven," counted Augustus to the sound of the bells hidden from sight in his hammock. "So it's,…half past seven?"

"Yes, Gusty," replied James Alexander Perry, having hoped to get at least a few more minutes' sleep before they were to report on deck.

Augustus ignored his hated nickname as Alexander resigned himself to waking up. Already, the morning felt lifeless. Alexander wished they were at sea where the waves could sway his hammock back and forth on its own. He twisted and threw his weight back and forth to try and recreate the familiar feeling. He couldn't stand the roughhewn wool of the hammock poking and irritating his skin. At least the gentle sway could help him to forget about it.

"Have you heard anything from your brother?" asked Henry Laub.

Alexander gave up on the swinging and propped himself up by his elbows. The berth was dark that morning. Their lone window looked to the West. Through the small opening he could see the distant line of trees that marked the borders of Put-in-Bay on the Southern edge of Lake Erie. He turned to Henry, disheveled hair and one arm hanging over the side of his cloth bedding, and said, "No, I haven't spoken to him in three days."

"What good is having the commodore's little brother as a fellow midshipman if you don't know any more than the rest of us?" Henry asked, his arm and head disappearing back into his hammock with only a tuft of wavy brown hair peeking out from the top.

"Is today the eleventh?" asked Augustus to the room, his voice rising from his hiding spot before he sat up for the first time.

Alexander turned to look at the ruddy faced New Yorker. He didn't know much about Augustus Swartwout except that his family was rich and that his father had bought his commission despite Augustus never having set foot in a boat before. "No, it's the ninth," replied Alexander as he wondered if he should ask the older boy what he was even doing on an American naval brig. It *was* easy to lose track of time on board he quietly admitted to himself. Alexander had heard that normal 12 year olds spend their time wandering through the woods and fishing by little rivers instead of on war ships.

A loud snore from the fourth inhabitant of the room, Dulaney Forest, interrupted Alexander's train of thought. They were all four of them midshipmen, with a fifth, Peleg Dunham, currently on deck as officer of the watch. Alexander was the youngest of them and Dulaney the oldest. Most, save Augustus, had been on ships their whole lives. They all served as junior officers to Lieutenant John Yarnell who reported to Commodore Oliver Hazard Perry, Alexander's older brother.

The sixteen-year-old Dulaney's leg hung lazily from the hammock as he shifted around in the wool cloth. He and Alexander had become fast friends when they first met in Erie, Pennsylvania a few months ago as the ship in which they slept, the USS <u>Lawrence</u>, and its sister ship, the USS <u>Niagara</u>, were being built. Dulaney had seen more naval action in battles and skirmishes than anyone on the ship save the commodore himself, and he could sleep through almost anything while waking at a moment's notice, ready to do his duty. He'd sleep until their watch started at eight bells and still be on deck before he was needed, somehow. Henry threw a small book at the snoring midshipman, hitting his foot, who drowsily rubbed his close cut hair, turned on his side, and continued sleeping soundly.

"I need a bath," said Augustus to no one in particular. He sniffed at his coat which he had slept in and gagged slightly.

"We all stink, Gusty," said Henry, getting up and swinging out of his hammock and onto the cold wooden floor.

"You could jump into the lake," added Alexander thinking that it wasn't a terrible idea, while also wishing that Augustus hadn't said anything. The wool of his own hammock seemed to have pooled the stench of sweat and grease into one powerful and offensive odor. He had managed to ignore it through the morning, but he couldn't escape it now except by actually getting up. He threw his legs out from the bedding and jumped onto the cool deck below. His bare feet tried to rebel, wanting nothing more than to retreat back under the coarsely warm woolen blanket, but Alexander's mind was in command, and determined to leave the putrid smell behind. But something was wrong, terribly wrong. His boots and socks were gone. Missing. Nowhere to be found.

"Lose something?" asked Henry wily as he removed his hammock from its hooks in the ceiling.

"Where are my boots?" Alexander sniped back. The floor was getting no warmer and his feet only colder. He began to dance back and forth, trying to keep his feet off of the cold wood.

"Tell me what you know."

"Know about what? Where are my boots?" Alexander felt more and more desperate with every passing second.

"The commodore must have told you something about the person who came on board last night," replied Henry, tossing his hammock into storage.

"He hasn't told me anything. I haven't seen him," replied Alexander, remembering the mysterious footsteps and indistinct murmurings that had gone on above them in the middle of the night.

"They're over there," added Augustus, pointing to the footwear partially hidden by a coat underneath the window.

As Alexander jumped towards his boots Henry said, "You're no fun," to Augustus and left the berth to go on deck.

Alexander covered his feet with his socks, swearing to never sleep without them again, and rubbed his cold toes. After a moment he looked up to the ruddy-faced midshipman from New York and said, "Thank you." He felt bad for using the nickname earlier.

A small smile escaped Augustus's lips as he took up his pencil from his lap and scratched a bit in his book. "You're welcome," he replied without looking up.

Alexander scrunched up his toes firmly planted in his socks and boots, trying to warm them faster. He walked over to Dulaney's snoring head, stared at him for a moment, wondering if the midshipman was actually asleep, and rapped his knuckles against the unconscious forehead. Dulaney snorted, mindlessly rubbed the close cut head, and became still one again. Augustus tried to suppress a snort of laughter. Alexander put his finger to his lips and began to rock the hammock back and forth. Augustus covered his mouth with his hand as the swing grew larger. Alexander wasn't sure if he'd take it as far as he could when he started, but the audience of one only encouraged him further until he pushed Dulaney so far that he tumbled out of the hammock and onto the floor. Augustus burst into laughter as Dulaney began to curse wildly.

After a moment of disorientated bumbling, Dulaney found his feet and the prankster standing before him. Alexander stood steadily before the older boy, sure of his safety.

"Eight bells," Alexander said calmly.

"What? When?" demanded Dulaney.

"Twenty minutes."

Panic streaked across Dulaney's face. "Have I slept in?"

"No. It's still twenty minutes away."

"Rhode Island rat," replied Dulaney under his breath, obviously fighting back the desire to strike the commodore's baby brother. "If you weren't Perry's little brother…"

"Really?" interrupted Alexander. "You'd treat me differently?" Alexander enjoyed this.

The angry frown on Dulaney's face melted away and was replaced by a knowing smirk. "You got me good," he said slapping Alexander on the arm. "Watch out, though," Dulaney rocked Alexander back and forth with his hand on the boy's shoulder. They smiled at each other as Alexander became wary of what he had gotten himself into. "Go on deck."

Alexander nodded to Dulaney, waved to Augustus, suppressed the fear of Dulaney's reprisal, and walked out of the berth where he bounded up the stairs to the open air. It had been a warm autumn so far, and the leaves were only just beginning to turn their yellows, reds, and browns on all of the trees that surrounded Put-in-Bay. Alexander walked to the starboard taffrail and leaned over it, breathing in deeply the distant smell of pine mixed with the fresh water lake around him.

He ran his fingers across the grain of wood and looked Eastward towards Lake Ontario. As Alexander imagined flying over the wilderness to that other Great Lake, he saw Commodore Chauncey in his mind's eye fighting the British Commodore Sir Yeo over the water. He peered into those British vessels and tried to pick out the Americans who the British had impressed into service for the crown. All of the midshipmen on the Lawrence knew at least one man who had been stolen from their homes and livelihood to work the galleys, so to speak. It was why America was fighting.

Alexander turned Southeast, past the hundreds of miles of wilderness, past Philadelphia to Washington City and the President's Mansion where James Madison conducted the war. The boy had heard that Mr. Madison was a short man and that Alexander was probably taller than him. People called him the Father of the Constitution. Alexander knew that

Mr. Madison might not be a tall man, but that he would stand tall in history.

Still, Alexander peered further East to distant England and the Court of St. James where sat King George III. That man who America had tossed aside a generation ago was still trying to dictate America's destiny, ordering Americans to man British ships in the service of his war with Napoleon.

As Alexander came back West, his eye rested on Newport, Rhode Island, his home. There, he saw his house and mother. His mother, Sarah, held Alexander's younger brother Nathaniel in her lap, telling him tales of naval glory. Those same tales were the ones she had told Alexander and Oliver before him. Tales of the Drake during the Revolution and the burning of the Philadelphia during the Barbary War were probably supplemented with Oliver's exploits as a junior officer on the General Greene from the Quasi-War thirteen years before.

Returning his mind to the deck of the Lawrence, Alexander scanned the entire American fleet laying anchored in the shallow water. The tall mainmast of the Niagara, commanded by Captain Jesse Elliott, towered over the smaller masts of the Caledonia, the Ariel, the Scorpion, and the Somers. There were three other ships (the Tigress, the Porcupine, and the Trippe), but they were all resting behind the Niagara, hidden by her rigging. Together, they represented the greatest collection of naval power the United States had ever assembled in so small a place under a single purpose. Running his fingers along the grain of the ship's hull, Alexander could almost feel the pent up power of the vessel that carried him, the twenty guns that defended her, and the dozens of sailors that manned her. Her hemp ropes intertwined above her hull, twisting back and forth and up and down. With the sails tucked tightly away at the booms that crossed the masts, the effect was almost like an unopened package, a gift of fury, waiting for its recipient.

He looked beyond the fleet, though. Over the calm autumn water of Lake Erie Alexander's mind glided until he saw the enemy. Amidst the sloops and schooners towered the Detroit, the newly completed British brig, larger than any American ship in hundreds of miles. Her completion meant that the two weeks of inaction and boredom in Put-in-Bay could come to a crashing end at any time. On her quarter deck by the pilot's wheel Alexander imagined Commodore Robert Barclay who had fought with the legendary British Admiral Lord Horatio Nelson at the Battle of Trafalgar against the French where Barclay had lost an arm during the fighting and Lord Nelson had lost his life in victory.

Those stories of great triumphs never told of the endless days performing perfunctory tasks, however, and yet that's all that Alexander had known for weeks now, and would probably know for at least one more day.

With only a few minutes to eight, the midshipmen began to line up at the pilot's station, waiting for their morning's orders. Alexander fell in line as the third followed soon thereafter by Peleg Dunham, the fourth, and then Dulaney as the last midshipman, whose uniform hung straighter and cleaner than any of the others. A few moments later the boatswain, Joseph Cheeves, came up from the gundeck. Cheeve's face was marked by decades at sea. Looking windward for years of his life had pot marked his cheeks like the remnants of smallpox. He only had nine fingers, one being lost to an errant rope on one of his early voyages. He squinted wherever he looked and couldn't quite stand up straight from so much time below deck. Alexander had known many faces like his back at Newport, and his own father carried some of the same features. For just a moment, Alexander wished for home.

Cheeves, as was his morning routing, held the daily list of duties that the captain had signed off on earlier that morning. "Mr. Laub," he snapped, calling the first midshipman's name, "to the deck this morning. Mr. Perry, up the mast. The captain wants an inspection of every sail. Mr. Forrest and Mr. Dunham to the guns. Clean as a whistle now. And Mr. Swartwout, the captain wants the boats scrubbed. He doesn't want a bump when he climbs in one."

For a moment, no one moved. A gaggle of seamen had gathered quietly on the quarterdeck below. The boatswain turned around and shouted, "Snap to it, you dogs! You know your places."

The ship was suddenly a beehive of activity as Newport sailors knocked aside Kentucky backwoodsmen who had a harder time remembering where their assignments took them.

Dulaney held Alexander's arm for a moment and asked, with his eyes scanning the bustle around them, "Do you think the captain will drill us on the guns again today?"

"I'd be surprised if he didn't do it twice," replied Alexander, looking up at the taller officer.

Disappointment and pain swam across the older boy's face as he removed his stovepipe hat, rubbed his head, and said, "I was hoping for a little break from the smoke."

"How daft are you?" asked Henry Laub, briefly leaning into the conversation. "With the enemy so close?" He turned to the men on the quarterdeck and shouted, "Get to work!"

"Well," said Dulaney to Alexander, "so it is." He paused and looked up to the rigging. "Don't fall today, squirt."

"Don't accidentally shoot your head off, old man."

The two junior officers parted, one ascending to the clear heavens and the other to mingle with iron.

Alexander commanded eight men. Two were from Newport, Henry Stephens and Peter Kinsley, Alexander had known them by name for years although he had never met or spoken to them before the days on the Lawrence. These two were already halfway up the mast, climbing with their bare feet grasping the wooden pole. Four were from Kentucky and climbed much more slowly, grasping to the netting that extended from the taffrail up to the boom. Charles Pohig, the seventh, from Charleston, was a man who had served on merchant vessels and privateers since he was a boy fifteen years ago. The eighth was probably the most interesting man on the ship. He was a Russian, but no one knew his real name. They all called him Ivan since it was the first Russian name someone on board had come up with. He seemingly spoke no English, although he apparently understood the language well enough. He could follow any order without hearing it again, but he always responded with a half-slurred, "Ya!" He was a good seaman, probably one of the best across the entire squadron, but it was because of his anger that the midshipmen loved him. His curses, while completely incomprehensible, sounded so colorful and lasted for so long that Alexander usually forgot what the old Russian was mad about due to the sustained laughter. It also helped that Ivan's head was half bald with stringy unkempt white hair that dangled limply to his shoulders and eyes set so far forward in his face that Alexander wondered whether they would pop out with a stiff knock to the back of the head.

Alexander followed his Newport brethren straight up the mast. As he went up, the gentle breeze flipped his hair over his eyes, but Alexander stayed calm. He could climb a mast like this in the dark of a moonless night. He gained the crow's nest and looked down and the myriad faces that made up the compliment of the USS Lawrence. Alexander's crew was a motley sort, but his men were no different from the rest of the fleet. They were a hodgepodge mix of Northerners, Southerners, freemen, natives, foreigners, and even a former slave, and yet, through the firm hand of Commodore Perry, they worked together, lived together, and became friends together on a collection of tiny floating villages creating a single cohesive fleet.

After telling Johnson, one of the Kentucky men, how to properly untie the rope that bound the sail, Alexander thought again of the fleet on the other side of the water. He could only guess at the composition of the crew of the British vessels. Most likely the men were veterans of many of the same battles as their commodore, Barclay, and his officers certainly were. Peering into the clear distance, Alexander thought he could make out the distant shore. The British had more guns, more men, and more experience he was sure, but he was also sure that the Americans had Oliver Hazard Perry. A few weeks earlier, with the enemy only a mile away, Oliver had coolly directed the dangerous movement to cross the high sandbars outside of Erie, Pennsylvania. Alexander had watched and followed orders in awe as the Commodore first ordered all of the smaller ships that could clear the sandbar over and to act as a nuisance to the nearby enemy ships and then to empty the two American brigs, the Lawrence and the Niagara, of everything so their keels could pass safely over the four-foot-deep passage. The British should have been able to pick apart the defenseless and nearly motionless flagship, but the Commodore's orders had kept them at bay.

With a deep rumble and heavy flutter, the men released the sail. The cloth was so untouched by wind, rain, and all manner of Nature's wrath that it gaily bounced the light into Alexander's eyes, blinding him for just a moment. By the time Alexander had recovered his vision, the Newport men were already standing sideways on the horizontal yard that had held the sail as though the Earth had turned wrong and made left and right into up and down. They hung there naturally defying gravity with tightly wrapped hemp gripping them around their waists.

"How does it look?" shouted Alexander, trying to deepen his voice and add some more authority to his words.

"She looks good, sir. I don't see anything," replied Stephens.

"Aye, sir. Like a maiden," said Kinsley, turning his head to the midshipman. "No tears. No holes. Nothing."

"Wh...what kind of maiden?" said Johnson, gripping the yard with both arms without hazarding to look down. He was trying to put himself at ease so far off the ground it seemed. His feet were firmly in place in the netting, but his arms clung tightly to the wood.

"As pretty as your sister," said Stephens with a chuckle which most of the men mirthfully followed.

"Ca...can't be *that* bad, can it?" replied Johnson, tightening his grip after a small breeze sent the netting swaying slightly.

They all broke into a hearty laugh with Johnson's rejoinder, including Alexander. He needed to take a moment to collect himself before he could straighten up and rediscover his "officer's voice", as Dulaney called it.

"Enough of that, then. Bring up the sail. We have about ten more to check."

The morning passed monotonously. One bell. 8:30. Check one sail. Check another sail. Two bells. 9:00. Check the fourth, fifth, and so on. Up one mast, back down, and up again until both masts had all of their sails cleared. They weren't all pristine. Half of them had small holes that needed quick patching made by birds looking for nesting material, but there were no serious issues. By six bells they had finished and Alexander set them to scrubbing the mast when he saw Dulaney waving him down.

Alexander bounded down the mast and landed surefooted, his boots thudding against the wood, near the older midshipman.

"He's drilling us at seven bells," said Dulaney.

"How do you know?"

"The lieutenant let slip."

Alexander had really hoped for lunch before the drilling began.

"Don't forget," Dulaney added, "you're officer of the watch next."

Alexander *had* forgotten. Firing the guns was exhausting work, and following that up with four hours in charge of the ship, even anchored safely in the bay, was a taxing chore. Administration was another reality of sailing life that always seemed to get left out of the adventure stories of Alexander's youth. Ensuring that all of the crew, the quartermaster, boatswain, and the lookouts were actually doing their jobs took a mental effort that he knew would be challenging after a drill. If by some miracle, his brother or Lieutenant Yarnall weren't onboard it would be somewhat easier since they could let up on the men a bit more. However, with the commanding officers present, Alexander could tolerate no slack. Maybe Oliver would give some lessons today and relieve Alexander of his duties for at least an hour in order to attend.

The quick drumming that marked a surprise drill suddenly shattered the quiet and calm on deck as though they were all of a sudden under attack. Without a word, both Dulaney and Alexander moved to their guns and marked their places by their thirty-two pound cannons as their guncrews worked their ways towards them through everyone else's preparations. All four Kentucky men were in charge of the tackle to the two thirty-two's (which they had named Raisin at the behest of the Kentucky men and the General Greene after Commodore Perry's first vessel). The two men on the Raisin began pulling uselessly at their ropes the second they arrived at the gun, trying to get the guns into firing position. Ivan quickly cursed in Russian, knocked aside the wooden blocks at the wheels that kept the guns in place, and smacked the closest Kentucky man (Mr. Frederick) on the back of the head. Mr. Kinsley was the loader on the General Greene and Mr. Stephens was the same on the Raisin. Mr. Schroeder, the other man from Newport, and Ivan were in charge of priming and firing the guns once loaded.

After the initial mix-up the process moved smoothly. The loaders shoved the wadding and balls. The tackle men pulled the ropes to get the guns to extend past the taffrail, and the primers readied the triggers. From the moment all eight men had arrived, gathered at the guns in the cramped starboard quarter of the gundeck, to finishing the loading and waiting for the order to fire was a respectable minute and fifty seconds or so. They had certainly done better in the past, and Alexander was certain that they would do better in the future, but for the moment, the midshipman simply nodded approvingly to his two guncrews and waited.

Quiet fell again on deck after every crew stood ready (Augustus's crew finished last). A moment later, however, with the order to lose the cannons, that quiet instantly turned into a deafening clamor which then turned to a dull ringing in Alexander's ears. It would pass, it always did, but it made giving and receiving orders much more difficult. Thankfully, the men knew what to do. Without any audible orders, the loaders gathered up their materials and pushed them down the chambers of the guns which had been pushed back from the taffrail by the force of the blast, the primers readied the triggers, and the tackle men pulled the cannons back into position, all while Alexander counted the time in his head. Soon enough (about a minute and thirty seconds later) his crews stood ready, straining to hear the lieutenant's command above the ringing. Alexander didn't hear the order, but he heard the dull thud of the guns closest to the lieutenant. Instinctively, Alexander patted both of the primers on their backs as he shouted "Fire!" as loudly as he could, hoping that they could hear him.

Acrid smoke filled the air yet again. Alexander's eyes burned and watered, his lungs began to strain, and he could barely see or hear anything. If his brother had not drilled them so much over the past months, the young midshipman would have been lost in the haze. However, Alexander knew what was next. He looked up, peering through the slowly clearing smoke to Lieutenant Yarnall who continued to shout orders. Alexander couldn't make out much, but just enough to verify that they were running out the port guns as well. Everyone else knew it too and sprinted the twenty feet to the opposite cannons. With a clip and increased efficiency they repeated the exercise. His own crew never got better than one minute and twenty-five seconds between firings, but it was still quite respectable.

The undertaking soon ended and the crews went back to work (many clearing the mess the exercise had created). Eight bells, noon, and the end of the forenoon watch, had passed during the firing, and Yarnall expected Alexander on the quarterdeck to take up his duties. He made his way up into the fresh air and blue sky. It was almost like heaven after the trial below, but he didn't have time to revel in the feeling. Instead of being able to lean over the taffrail to take in a deep breath of clean air, he walked up to Lieutenant Yarnall who stood erect at the ship's helm next to William Steers, the Lawrence's pilot. Yarnall was maybe twenty years old, not much older than Dulaney, but he seemed to fill the space he stood in more completely than any of the midshipmen despite his narrow frame. Alexander thought he looked more like a store clerk than a sailor. Perhaps it was the handsome hat that rested comfortably atop his head, but despite his high-pitched voice, he still commanded respect from all men on ship. No matter what is was, though, Alexander had felt a need to understand it better for some time.

"Good afternoon, Lieutenant," said Alexander.

"Good afternoon, Mr. Perry," Yarnall replied. "Two minutes past noon."

"I'm sorry, sir." Alexander made no attempt to offer an excuse. They both knew that the drill had gone a little long and that the observation was far from a formal rebuke. "It won't happen again."

"See that it doesn't," replied the lieutenant almost placidly as he wound his pocket watch and slipped it back into his coat.

"Yes, sir."

"Clear day. I left our positioning to you, Mr. Perry."

"Yes, sir. Thank you, sir."

Lieutenant Yarnall began to walk away.

"Sir?" asked Alexander, feeling the familiar nervousness in his stomach he experienced when asking something of his superior officer.

"What can I do for you, Mr. Perry?" asked Yarnall with a friendly smile almost escaping his lips.

"Has…has there been any news? I thought I heard someone come aboard last night."

The half-hidden smile faded. Gone was the store clerk. For that moment, Alexander saw the hardened seaman. Alexander could feel the curious eyes of Mr. Steers bore through him as Yarnall's look darted from the pilot to the midshipman. After a moment of thought, Yarnall said,

"Commodore Perry will share any news at dinner."

"Yes, sir," replied Alexander, trying to hide his disappointment.

"Very good. Is there anything else that you need, Mr. Perry, or may I continue with my own duties?"

"Of course not, sir. Sorry, sir."

Lieutenant Yarnall nodded to the young midshipman as he turned back to descend the stairs to the poop deck. The seamen in front of him moved out of his way and saluted as he passed. Alexander walked to the taffrail and looked out to the forests across the water. He remembered what Henry had said earlier and asked himself what good *was* it being the commodore's brother if he couldn't learn anything more than any other junior officer? He had imagined that serving on Oliver's ship would provide some benefits, but there was nothing. He was just another midshipman.

CHAPTER II: Tales Told at Sea

Bataille des Saintes by Thomas Whitcombe

"Mr. Steers, do you have the sextant ready?" Alexander said to the pilot when he turned back towards his duties.

"Yes, sir," Steers mumbled as he turned to the storage trunk by the gunwale and pulled out the bronze device. It was a piece of equipment Alexander had long been familiar with. He had peered through the telescopic eyepiece and measured latitude many times on land and at sea. Taking the hefty apparatus in his right hand, he peered around the ship to find the best place to see both the sun and the horizon. Once found on the starboard side, Alexander made sure the filter on the eyepiece was in place before he put it to his eye and found the sun. Using long familiar motions, he measured the angle between the sun and the horizon and performed the calculations in his head. 41°55' by 82°14'. The same as yesterday, Alexander thought, sighing. Mr. Steers had the log book open, ready for Alexander to record the reading. He took up the pen and looked over the page, and then flipped back two pages to find the last time the reading had varied. They had been sitting there in that spot in Put-in-Bay for seemingly forever. Looking at the log Alexander could see the boredom that he had been feeling. He flipped back and wrote their position in that day's log.

With the log book stuffed back into the trunk, Alexander put the pilot to scrubbing and cleaning parts of the quarterdeck that were already clean. Sitting idle for two weeks meant that very little maintenance was necessary to keep up the ship. Discipline, especially among the Kentucky men, was becoming sloppy. They could only scrub and swab a clean deck so many times before irritation set in. Frustration was evident in all of their eyes, but it was amazing to see it disappear whenever the Commodore emerged from his cabin and walked past. It wasn't just his presence, but his bearing and how he treated the men almost as equals that so effortlessly lifted their spirits amidst the man-made doldrums.

Dulaney was on the poop deck below directing the seamen there to scrub and clean the remains of smoke and grit left over from their drilling. After instilling some diligence into their work he bounded up to the quarterdeck to join Alexander.

"Sir," said Dulaney with a smirk and a half-hearted salute.

The two were technically the same rank, but Dulaney, in practice, outranked Alexander. The older midshipman was actually due to take the lieutenant's exam in a few months. And yet, it was in Dulaney's nature to easily josh the Commodore's little brother, feigning deference to the younger officer.

Dulaney tossed an apple to Alexander and leaned against the gunwale, keeping an eye on the deck scrubbing below while joining the officer of the deck.

"I think something may be about to happen," said Alexander after he wiped away the juice from his first bite, his mouth still full of the crunchy fruit.

"Oh? What gives you that idea?"

"Yarnall. He seemed a bit more…agitated than normal. When I asked about the noise from last night he said Oli…the commodore would tell us at dinner."

"Orders? Do you think Chauncey ordered us to attack? Or…the enemy is trying to make it to the Hudson?" Dulaney asked in a whisper, referring to Commodore Chauncey, on Lake Ontario two hundred miles away, preventing the British invasion of New York.

"Chauncey's been ordering us to attack for weeks," replied Alexander, remembering his brother's strenuous written pleas, which had become common knowledge on the ship, for more sailors to man the ship. That was why there were so many backwoods Kentuckians on board. Most had never been on more than a river craft in their lives, much less handled the complex rigging that made up a brig's sails. They were the Kentucky militiamen who were willing to follow their commanders past their state borders, which, by law, they were under no obligation to do. After many days and weeks of drilling and teaching, they had begun to learn the workings of a naval vessel of the United States. Most of the men in any sort of leadership were either Newport men or had been at sea in merchants or even warships akin to the <u>Lawrence</u>. The manpower problem was well known, but relief had arrived with Captain Jesse Elliot back in July. The fifty men Elliott had brought with him told tales of Elliott's bravery last October when he had captured two British vessels. Some of these same men grumbled that he should have been made commodore of the squadron when they had arrived to reinforce the forces on Lake Erie, preferring their own commander to the young Perry. Still, Commodore Perry had joyously given Elliott command of the <u>Lawrence</u>'s sister ship, the <u>Niagara</u>, and ever since that July evening, the rambunctious spirit of the fleet had grown. Dulaney and Alex weren't the only ones hoping to finally get into the fight.

"I can't imagine we'd still be at anchor if we'd gotten orders to attack with our compliment," said Dulaney.

"Maybe you're right. I guess we'll see at dinner."

Dulaney took one final bite from his own apple and tossed the already browning core as hard as he could at the forested coastline a few thousand feet away. The bit of fruit splashed into the bay with a plop, disappeared for a moment, and then bobbed up and down, slowly making its way to shore.

"I managed to read some more of that book last night," Dulaney said as he watched the core float away.

Alexander's eyes lit up. Dulaney had been reading a book of naval battles and had promised to lend it to Alexander as soon as he had finished, but Dulaney was s slow reader who'd rather sleep an extra thirty minutes than read a book late into the night.

"Did you read about Trafalgar?" asked Alexander, hoping to hear of Lord Nelson, the famous British admiral, and his victory over the French a decade ago.

"No, not yet. I did read about the Battle of the Saintes."

Everyone knew about Sir George Rodney's victory over the Comte de Grasse in the Caribbean. It had been the largest battle of the American Revolution, but funnily enough there hadn't been an American vessel present.

"Well?" asked Alexander. "Tell me about it."

"You remember how Rodney broke the French fleet's line?"

"Affleck did it too," interjected Alexander, happy to show off his knowledge of the engagement. There was always an implicit competition to see who knew more about naval history. The commodore encouraged it saying that they could never know when some detail of some battle might become useful.

"Right, well, the book had a description of the wind during the battle, and I suddenly can't decide if the battle was won because of Rodney's leadership or because of dumb luck. If the wind hadn't suddenly changed, both fleets would have probably kept raking each other at pistol shot until the sun went down."

Alexander thought for a moment, imagining a pair of mighty vessels with dozens of cannons each pouring metal into each other at 50 yards. "Maybe it's because of how many of the English captains saw the opportunity?"

"Two. Rodney and Affleck."

"Out of how many?"

"I don't know…a couple dozen?"

"And the French, what did they do?"

"I think the most they could have done was either try to close the gaps in their line, which the wind wouldn't let them do, or break their line themselves to match the British course. I don't think it would have worked, though."

"Maybe not."

"So what is it, then? Luck that the wind turned in just the right way so that Rodney could take advantage, or Rodney's skill?"

Their conversation was cut short by the retching sounds and rancid smell of a sailor vomiting onto the very wood he had been cleaning. Bilious fever had been running rampant through the ship's crew (nearly a third of the hundred men had done the same), and with each new case the crew lost a man capable of fighting.

"Sailor!" Alexander shouted at the sick seaman.

The kneeling man pushed himself up to look at the young midshipman, managing a queasy, "Yes, sir?"

"Go below and report to Dr. Parsons."

"Aye," the sailor replied as he collected his fallen cap, wiped his chin with his sleeves, and stumbled down the stairs.

"That's one more," said Alexander.

"One less. Will we even have enough to man the guns?" asked Dulaney to the breeze.

Alexander remembered how the crew looked up to Commodore Perry. Their eyes brightened as he asked them to work harder and faster. Alexander had seen it at Erie during the construction of the sister brigs. He had seen it in the mad dash over the sand bar. He had felt it then, too. He knew that he would feel it again when they entered battle.

"He'll fight. They'll all fight," said Alexander quietly. "With Oliver leading them, they'll fight."

"They will, won't they? They'd follow Commodore Perry into the mouths of Hell if he asked them," said Dulaney.

It was true, but Alexander wasn't sure why. His brother was an expert seaman and knew every aspect of sailing. He had seen action in the Caribbean and Mediterranean. He expected so much from everyone, but he treated them like his own kin. He was younger than many of the crew, but they still seemed to see him as a second father. It was all enough to convince men to follow him into battle, but Alexander didn't think it could be enough for the nearly fanatical devotion he thought he saw. While still at the Erie, some sailors from Newport had challenged some visiting militia men to a duel for disparaging the commodore. Perry had shut down the notion with some harsh words for the men, but they only thought more of him for it.

"Six bells," said Dulaney as the tones sounded across the ship. "Another hour on watch. Keep 'em working."

"Aye, sir," replied Alexander.

Dulaney walked down the stairs, side-stepped the vomit, and shouted at a pair of sailors who were idly talking instead of cleaning up the mess.

The final hour passed slowly. The afternoon was growing long and the warm day was beginning to change to a cool evening. When Henry Laub relieved Alexander of command, he happily let his fellow midshipman take it. They exchanges some pleasantries before Alexander quitted the quarterdeck, breathing deeply. The air suddenly tasted sweeter on his lips.

At the bottom of the stairs sat Hannibal Collins, a big black old salt whose giant hands were coiling rope for storage. Alexander had always found Hannibal to be fascinating. Slavery was still technically legal in Rhode Island, but it was steadily phasing out. Alexander wasn't even sure if he had ever seen one of the few remaining slaves in the state, and Hannibal Collins had been one of them at one point but not for more than ten years. He seemed to love liberty more than anyone else Alexander had ever met. He was also one of the only men on board who remembered anything about the American War for Independence. He had been in his teens when the British troops finally left their former colonies. Alexander wasn't sure if he believe Hannibal's story about him being at the very front row during the reading of the Declaration of Independence, but he certainly believed Hannibal's story about seeing George Washington.

"When he was first president," as Hannibal told it, "George Washington came to New England. I was still a slave, and no more than twenty years old, when I travelled with my master to Boston to see the Father of the Country. I was but one of thousands who watched the president talk a bit at the Long Lane Meeting House. As the president was making his way to his carriage, someone pushed me, sending me to the pavement near his feet." He paused in his telling as though still collecting himself from the fall. "Washington, after I was back to my feet, asked me if I was well before giving me a respectful nod and continuing on his way." One might consider the tale a flight of fancy, but Alexander was convinced that it was true because of how Hannibal was while he told it. Hannibal had a way of flailing his arms about as he told stories, gesturing with imaginary swords and threatening imaginary men, but not this one. This story he told very solemnly, as though he was reading from the Bible. Hannibal's reverence of George Washington sometimes seemed to border on the profane, especially telling that story.

But at that moment on deck, Hannibal was approaching another type of profanity as he sang a bawdy song about a woman from Georgia who had come to Boston. It was a song that Alexander had heard a dozen times before and enjoyed despite himself, but he saw Lieutenant Yarnall eyeing him from across the deck.

"Mr. Collins!" Alexander shouted, knowing that such bawdiness shouldn't be encouraged on board much less while on duty.

"Aye, sir?" asked Hannibal, spinning around with a quick salute. His look of consternation disappeared when he realized who was speaking to him, replaced by a small wave and a knowing smile.

"I think we've had quite enough of that, don't you think?" said Alexander, tilting his head towards the lieutenant, hoping that Hannibal would recognize him as no more than an errand boy for the order.

"Of course, sir," replied Hannibal, his smile broadening slightly. With a wink he continued, "Perhaps something more…patriotic?"

"Aye, that sounds fine."

Hannibal began singing "Yankee Doodle Dandy" until Lieutenant Yarnall turned his attention elsewhere. After a few more bars, Hannibal dropped his voice and addressed Alexander. "Mr. Perry, have you heard anything?"

"Maybe," replied Alexander, fully aware that he was being too friendly with a subordinate. "Well, nothing definitive, but I think something is about to happen, why?"

"I heard," said Hannibal, dropping to one knee and very slowly coiling more rope, "I heard that the captain is ordering a boat to go to all the other ships. It's supposed to be ready by five o'clock…two bells."

Alexander couldn't think of very many reasons Commodore Perry would send a single man to every ship in the fleet. The most obvious answer, orders to set sail, was also the one he had been dreaming of for some days now, so he found himself distrusting the notion. And yet, his gut wouldn't listen to the doubts in his head.

"What are you thinking, Mr. Perry?"

Alexander was about to respond when he looked back at the quarterdeck and saw Lieutenant Yarnall eyeing him again.

"Don't dawdle now," said Alexander to Hannibal with a stealthy wink.

Hannibal was soon back to singing "Yankee Doodle Dandy". It took Alexander a moment to realize that Hannibal had been using altered lyrics that turned the song into one about Americans stealing British women and showing them was true men were like. Yarnall seemed to notice at the same time and shouted, "Oi! Mr. Collins!" after which Hannibal returned to the original words.

Alexander sauntered up to the front of the ship. Giving orders as he went ("You call that a bowline? It won't hold. Do it again."), the young midshipman wanted to look out onto the fleet. The fore was empty and freshly scrubbed, and the ship seemed quieter from the front of the ship. The shouts of orders and thud of steps fell to the background as a pair of black-beaked grosbeaks, hopping up and down on the bowsprit, their red chests heaving up and down as they chirped at the late afternoon day. Before Alexander's eyes laid the entire squadron, all eight ships that answered to the <u>Lawrence</u>. Most were small schooners that held only two guns each. Looking at them in the shadow of the <u>Niagara</u> made them look even smaller than Alexander had thought of them at dock. They were important, but any battle would pivot around the sibling vessels built in Erie. If a battle were to come, there would be no escaping it on the <u>Lawrence</u>. They would be the focal point. His brother would be the prime target.

A new sound of creaking pulleys and straining rope rose from the deck behind the midshipmen drowning out the birdsong. Several sailors were moving a boat to lower it into the water below. Tall, composed Lieutenant Yarnall oversaw the action with the short and pudgy Augustus Swartwout next to him. Behind his back Yarnall held eight letters sealed with wax. Without a word, Alexander joined Dulaney, Henry Laub, and

Peleg Dunham next to Augustus.

"What is it? What's going on?" asked Alexander nudging Peleg.

"Gusty won't say," replied Peleg.

Augustus glared at Peleg for using his hated nickname.

"Augustus," said Alexander leaning over Peleg, "what is happening?"

The midshipmen from New York looked at Alexander and began to whisper, "I don't know, but..." when Lieutenant Yarnall coughed loudly, eyeing the junior officers firmly and ending all discussion.

The officer remained silent as the boat made its final release from the <u>Lawrence</u> splashing into the water. The sailors descended into the craft and began to dig out the oars and prepare the dinghy for departure. Amidst the quiet stares and low murmurings of the slowly gathering crew, Yarnall handed the letters to Augustus.

"Be quick about it, Mr. Swartwout. Commodore Perry would like you back in time for supper."

"Yes, sir," said Augustus with a wary smile and a quick salute. The smile disappeared, however, when he began to lower himself into the boat. He showed his greenness and seemed to find doing anything much more than standing still to be taxing. After Augustus had steadied himself into the boat and made way to the <u>Niagara</u>, Alexander, Henry, Peleg, and Dulaney turned to each other. Just looking into each other's eyes was enough to see that they all though the same thing.

Augustus held battle orders.

CHAPTER III: At the Commodore's Table

Portrait of Oliver Hazard Perry by Gilbert Stuart

Augustus returned to the <u>Lawrence</u>, having gone from ship to ship, handing the orders to each vessel's master. When he descended to the junior officer's berth the other young men questioned him relentlessly.

"What were in the letters?"

"Was it the order of battle?"

"I don't know. I couldn't read them. They were sealed."

"How did the captain react?"

"Did you see their eyes when they opened the orders?"

"Only Conklin and Packet opened them in front of me. Conklin didn't react, but Packet looked grave."

"Grave? What do you mean? Did he say anything?"

"No, he just thanked me and walked away."

"Well, did you get anything out of the commodore?"

"I haven't seen Captain Perry today. Yarnall called me over and told me I was delivering orders."

"Well? Could you read anything from him?"

"You know Yarnall. No one can read him."

Slowly, the midshipmen's excitement faded as it became more and more obvious that Augustus hadn't been able to gleam anything more from his task. The other officers, who had been crowding around him leaned back and rested against the walls of their shared cabin which had steadily darkened as the sun set.

Henry, sitting up in his hammock, swaying slightly back and forth with one hand pushing on the ceiling, studied Augustus's face, probably searching for a hidden clue, and addressed Alexander, "What do you think, Alex? Is your brother always like this before a fight?"

Alexander didn't know. He had never been in battle, much less with his older brother, but he couldn't admit it. He was the youngest and the most inexperienced midshipman, save Augustus, and yet they all held a certain deference to him because of his relationship to their commanding officer. Even Dulaney, who teased and prodded Alexander so often, would never actually try to hurt Alexander out of fear of the commodore. But, if Alexander lied and said he knew something, and it turned out to be wrong, he'd lose that little bit of respect. So Alexander thought quickly and found a way to sound authoritative without actually saying anything.

"He won't keep anything from us. I'm sure he'll tell us at dinner."

"You're probably right," replied Dulaney leaning back against the wall and picking at his nails.

"Is it time to go?" asked Peleg, patting his small belly. "I'm starving."

The midshipmen cleaned up as best they could, brushing off dirt, folding out creases, and putting on their dress coats before leaving their cabin and walking through the seaman's berth to the entrance of the captain's quarters. The cook's mate had already set out the simple wooden table and chairs and was busy placing the silverware on the table when the four young officers made their entrance. Alexander went as frequently as any of the other midshipmen, but they hardly ever went together. The captain's table was usually populated by Yarnall, William Taylor the sailing master, John Brooks the commander of the marines, Thomas Breese the chaplain, and Samuel Horsely the surgeon. Horsely, however, had been incapacitated by the bilious fever for some days now. Even then, adding all four midshipmen made the fit rather snug, although it was still certainly possible to squeeze such a large gathering in the cabin.

Taylor, the sailing master, was already there and stood talking to Thomas Breese the chaplain. A greater disparity between two physical forms of men would be hard to imagine. Taylor hunched over with his head awkwardly tucked to the side under the low ceiling was six foot three and looked like he had to bend over even to sit while below deck. He carried over three hundred pounds of fat, muscle, and experience on his tall frame and looked like he could devour the small man in front of him. That small man was no taller than five foot two and weighed no more than a hundred and twelve pounds, and yet it was the diminutive chaplain who seemed to dominate the conversation with a deep and echoing voice that did not match his body. He was a man of fifty with black and white muttonchops who had led so many different lives before his current post, all of which he made known through some ribald jokes he liked to tell, some being so scandalous that they would even embarrass the uncouth Hannibal Collins. Taylor was of a similar sort which was probably why they got along so handsomely. Whenever they were together, it was like they were in competition to see who could take the limits of decorum the furthest.

Soon entered John Brooks, commander of the marines to the cabin. At least six foot four but less imposing than Taylor, Brooks was a surprisingly quiet man outside of his official functions. Even within his duties, he was never boisterous, but only ever gave his orders with an even tone. His men were much like him, at least on duty. They were calm, quiet, but forceful. They made Alexander think of a sleepy bear that could become angry at the slightest provocation. At dinner Brooks rarely volunteered a word, but always spoke intelligently and well when called upon. Dipping his head to make his way into the captain's berth, Brooks carried his hat firmly against his side, and his outfit hugged his form so perfectly like he had just come from the tailor.

As Brooks greeted everyone in the room, barely registering in Taylor and Breese's conversation, he injected life into the midshipmen by simply asking some polite questions.

"I saw one of you feeding a bird earlier. Who was it?"

Peleg raised his hand slightly and replied, "I suppose that was me, sir."

"Often feed the birds?"

"Well, no, sir. I suppose I was just a bit bored."

"I suppose that we all can get a bit bored," agreed Brooks.

The junior officers nervously tried to move out of the way of the cook as he brought the dishes.

Usher Parsons, the acting surgeon walked in next. With Horsely sick, it was Parsons' responsibility to take up the knife. Although he had been through his own share of scrapes and adventures, this was probably his first time at Commodore Perry's table and yet he walked in as though he had been every night for a year, his head held high, his greying blonde hair brushing against the ceiling, shaking everyone's hand with fervor and confidence. The warm glow of candle light made the lake water in his thick yellow beard sparkle.

The entire party was gathered around the table save the two most senior officers, Lieutenant Yarnall and Commodore Perry himself. During the lulls of conversation, which were few and far between, Alexander could hear his brother's voice from behind the wooden partition that temporarily separated the cramped dining area from the commodore's desk. Soon enough, the cook's mate removed the partition, revealing Commodore Perry bent over charts of the lake with his lieutenant next to him reading out some numbers from a book in his hand. Perry's white and brown haired spaniel slept in the commodore's chair next to them.

Conversation died as the dinner party waited for its host. Perry's face was lined with concentration and worry, a look Alexander was surprisingly unfamiliar with. He thought he knew most of his older brother's moods, but this particular expression was definitely foreign. Oliver Perry was usually very jovial and open, a marked contrast to the studious and anxious air he bore at his desk. In that moment he looked forty-seven instead of twenty-seven.

The commodore stood up and straightened his shirt and coat as he noticed his guests and the previous look melted away revealing the personable and loving commander that they all knew.

"Welcome, gentlemen," Commodore Perry said almost jubilantly.

"Good evening, Commodore," everyone replied.

"Please, don't wait for me. Sit down and pour the wine," he said extending his arm in the direction of the table.

They all sat down while the senior officers finished their work. Taylor took it upon himself to pour the table's drinks, sending the cook's mate to help finish the meal. ("We're starving!" he shouted after the boy.) The conversation quickly continued along the previous lines with Taylor and Breese sucking most of the air from the room while Parsons and Brooks spoke politely to each other as they tried to involve the midshipmen to varying degrees of success. Dulaney happily chimed in much more comfortably than the rest. Henry, Peleg, and Augustus mostly spoke to each other, while Alexander watched and listened. After a couple more minutes Commodore Perry and Lieutenant Yarnall took their seats at the head of the table and its right hand respectively. Yarnall sat quietly while Perry butted in and finished the story Taylor had been telling to Breese ("He pulled it out of his pocket and shouted, 'How did that get there?'"). As the table laughed at both the story and Taylor's bemused but frustrated look, the cook entered the room with dinner.

"How foul, another fowl!" cried Taylor trying to regain some of his lost thunder.

Perry chuckled and shook his head as Breese said, "That was atrocious!"

Dinner was a swan that had been shot the previous day. Cooked with stuffing and gravy, it was a feast the like of which the midshipmen rarely had the pleasure of enjoying. They all gazed at the smoking brown bird, taking in the succulent smell as Perry stood up with the carving knife and a fork. Before he took the silver to the bird, however, he addressed his officers.

"I'm very pleased to have you all here for dinner, and I do deeply wish that this could be an evening just spent in your good company, but I'm afraid that naval matters *must* come first." He forcefully stuck the fork into the bird. "We have received intelligence that the enemy has begun patrolling the lake with its entire squadron." He paused. No one said a word. "And, seeing as the reinforcements brought by Captain Elliott have managed to fill out our ranks well enough, and after discussing matters with General Harrison, I have decided that we will weigh anchor tomorrow and sail to meet the enemy."

The room fell silent for a moment as the commodore stood upright and looked over his officers. Only the muted splashes of small waves hitting the hull and the creaking of wooden boards underfoot filled the silence.

"I have sent orders to every captain the squadron with the order of battle." He picked up his glass and held it up as a small credit to Augustus. "We will be out front to meet the Detroit. Following us will come the Caledonia, the Niagara, the Somers, the Porcupine, the Tigress, and then the Trippe with the Scorpion and Ariel acting as dispatch vessels. I have also given the captains information on the signal to move in for attack at close range. When the situation best suits us, I will order my new battle flag flown from the foremast. Some of you may have seen this new standard, which I commissioned while at Erie, but for those of you who haven't…"

Lieutenant Yarnall stood up and followed Perry to the commodore's desk. The dog woke up just long enough to note what was going on around him before laying his head back down upon his paws and looking at the crowd idly. The two senior officers grabbed a piece of blue cloth and unfurled it between them. Of all the things that Alexander had been privy to due to his relationship with the commodore, this had been kept from him. Five simple words written in white on a blue background was the entirety of the flag's design. "DONT GIVE UP THE SHIP" It was a phrase that everyone in that room, everyone on that ship, understood. Everyone knew about the flag, but until that moment no one had actually seen it. And yet, Alexander remembered the day the ladies of the Stewart family had come to the dockyard and given Commodore Perry the fruits of their labor based on his design. It was hard to forget the five beautiful women from about thirteen to their mid-twenties coming on board. The youngest one, whose name Alexander had never learned, had smiled at him.

"These are the words of my friend, James Lawrence, our vessel's namesake. He said these words, his last, three months ago as his ship, the Chesapeake, lost its battle against the enemy. I want all of us to remember these words. There is nothing more dangerous to our enemy and more powerful for our nation than a group of Americans who sail into battle ready to fight to the end. We all know, and even admire, the British prowess at sea, but as no Brit can stand toe to toe with an American, as the thousand British dead at Lexington prove, and as no man would have ever chose King *George* III," he said with a knowing smirk, "over General *George* Washington, so shall no British fleet triumph over an American squadron, especially in our own waters. What say you?"

Alexander's blood was up. He could have manned a gun at that very moment, and, looking around the table, he could see that he wasn't the only one. The large Taylor was beating his paw against the table, shaking the glasses, as he shouted, "Hear! Hear!" The chaplain clapped loudly. Even Commander Brooks seemed to be fighting a large reaction as he politely raised his glass.

"Enough talk, gentlemen," said Commodore Perry as Yarnall put up and folded the flag. "Shall we dine?"

Perry cut and served the swan. Glasses of wine emptied and everyone became merrier as the evening progressed. The dog, now fully awake, begged at the feet of every man at the table before finding that Peleg was the most willing to give him scraps from his own plate.

After more than an hour of stories and bragging, Commodore Perry suddenly shouted, "Oh, no!"

The table fell silent waiting to hear some awful news.

Perry looked around the table and began to laugh. "Forgive me, gentlemen. I didn't mean to frighten you. It's just that I remembered that I've been so busy today that I forgot to give our fine upstanding midshipmen their daily lesson."

Their lessons with the senior officers were the closest the midshipmen got to a school while in the service. Alexander generally enjoyed them, especially if his brother taught them. Commodore Perry was an easy, almost playful, teacher who managed to make even tedious lessons amusing. They tended to be more practical in nature than what Alexander had sat through in the schoolhouse in Newport. Knots, rigging, cannon maintenance, sail patterns, and the wind were far more immediate to Alexander's life than sums or civics.

"Well, good sirs, I am not prepared for anything specific, but if there's a subject on which you would like to learn, you have dozens of years of naval service here to answer you," said Perry indicating the senior officers.

The midshipmen looked at each other. They were as unprepared for this as anyone else at that table. The silence began to grow uncomfortable until Dulaney took the initiative and said, "Sir, Mr. Perry and I were discussing something earlier, and I was hoping to hear your opinion on it."

"Oh?" replied the commodore leaning over his plate, folding his hands, and looking Dulaney in the eye. "And what's that?"

"Well, sir, I've been reading a book on the famous naval battles of the last century, and the Battle of the Saintes left me questioning Rodney."

"And what, pray tell," asked Perry sardonically, "what does Mr. Dulaney Forest, midshipman, have to teach Admiral Sir George Rodney of the HMS Formidable?"

"No," replied Dulaney, sheepishly smiling, "It's nothing like that at all."

"Of course not," said Perry playfully as the other men chuckled. "So, what is it, then?"

This was a sight Alexander had never seen before: Dulaney disarmed rhetorically. The commodore was spirited, but something about him made the eldest midshipman anxious.

"Sir," interjected Alexander immediately regretting it as all eyes fixed on him.

"Yes, Mr. Perry," replied the commodore.

"I believe that Mr. Forrest is trying to say that he was unsure of whether Rodney's decision to break the enemy's line was a matter of leadership or of luck that the wind changed."

"A fine question!" boisterously shouted Taylor as he finished off his fifth glass of wine.

"Yes, yes it is," said Perry as he leaned back and inspected both midshipmen. "Tell me, Mr. Perry, on which side of the argument did you fall?"

"I said it was leadership, sir."

"And the wind had nothing to do with it, then? Can you lead men to walk through walls or fly through the air? Does Nature and Nature's God have no say in the matter?"

Alexander didn't know how to respond. He saw Dulaney smugly smiling at him, and suddenly Alexander became convinced that he had been wrong.

The commodore must have seen the same thing because he turned to Dulaney and asked, "And you, Mr. Forrest, do you think that any trick of the wind is enough to turn a battle completely on its head?"

Dulaney's smile vanished and he replied, "Uh…no sir?"

"I'd say that they boy might be beginning to get it," piped up Mr. Breese. The fact that the non-military man at the table seemed to understand embarrassed Alexander.

"Yes, perhaps," said Perry. "Tell me, do you know of many battles where conditions never changed? Where the initial plan followed through to the end without a hiccup? Where the captain's strategy never needed modification once the guns started to blaze? And not just at sea, but on land as well?"

No one spoke for a moment as the midshipmen racked their brains trying to find a single example.

"Well," continued Perry, "I'm sure that if you sat for years and read every book on the subject you could come up with a handful of examples. A handful against the thousands of battles that man has been fighting against his brother since Cain first hit Abel with a rock. No, young sir, winds shift, rain falls, and grounds quake. It is the nature of fighting real enemies instead of those in your head. But, the question is, are these natural events, some might even say divine interventions, enough to alter battles on their own? I say no. Do you agree Mr. Brooks?"

"Heartily, sir," said the marine softly but firmly.

"It takes men of vision and wit to see the changing circumstances, throw out all of his carefully laid plans, change course, and still come out victorious. All of these things Rodney did. He recognized not just the changing winds, but also what he needed to do to use that alteration and inflict the most damage upon the French fleet."

"But sir," interrupted Augustus, "if I remember correctly, didn't Rodney take his ship and cut directly into the enemy's path?"

"Yes, he did, Mr. Swartwout."

Augustus smiled broadly, his thick cheeks turning red. "I'm curious, sir, but why didn't the French see it coming and do something about it?" he asked.

"Very good question, Mr. Swartwout," replied Perry with a smile. He turned to the other midshipmen, "Can any of you give Mr. Swartwout the answer?"

A nervous silence fell on the table for a moment until Henry said, "Because it's too dangerous?"

"Very good! Can you explain why?"

"Well, sir," replied Henry looking down at his plate, "I think it's because it can be difficult to time correctly."

"Do look up at the men you address Mr. Laub, if you please. Now, do you know what can happen if that timing is incorrect?"

Henry didn't reply for a moment but looked at the Commodore as he thought.

"In Ancient Greece," said Perry addressing all of the junior officers and answering his own question, "navies mainly fought by ramming into each other, driving their bows into the sides of their enemies. The blows would cause minimal damage to the attacking ship but would cripple the one that receiving it. That same principle would apply to our frigates and brigs, except that our vessels were never designed for ramming, meaning that both ships, the attacking and the attacked, could sustain crippling damage. Breaking the line of your enemy suddenly puts you in danger of both hitting and being hit by the enemy."

"So," said Augustus looking the commodore in the eye, "why would anyone do it?"

"Can you imagine the damage you could inflict upon the enemy by firing almost completely unopposed on both sides of you?" Perry said with a smile. "Port hitting the aft of the ship at what had been the fore and starboard hitting the bow of the ship at what had been aft? In fact, that's exactly what happened when Rodney took the Formidable through the French line, eventually inflicting enough damage to incite the Comte de Grasse's surrender. Rodney saw the wind change and knew it was possible to steer his ship into cutting off the French, and then executed the action so well five more British ships were able to follow him. That was true leadership, young sirs, and I hope that you can learn from it."

"Perhaps you should have become a school master," said Parsons.

"Perhaps," replied Perry, raising his glass to the acting surgeon. "We'll see how tomorrow plays out first before we change my profession, though."

The rest of the dinner passed with a mixture of frivolity and ease that always managed to make dinners at Commodore Perry's table both enjoyable to the senior officers and equally terrifying to the young midshipmen. Trying to stifle laughter at some of the bawdier jokes by Taylor and Breese while the Commodore looked on with a gentle hint of disappointment in his eyes was no easy task for the junior officers who originally had no idea that some of Philadelphia's streets should be avoided to preserve one's own virtue. However, before Taylor could get too far into most of his sagas of wine, women, and song, Commodore Perry would politely cough, cut off the story, and take the conversation in a more modest direction, usually with a quick anecdote of Newport or naval daring.

As Taylor began one story dealing with a particular woman from Albany he stressed that he had never met but had, on good authority, created a drink that included a mummified toe, Perry stood up, interrupting his sailing master, and began to speak. The commodore's voice quickly drowned out all other noise, Taylor's own voice swiftly fading away.

"Gentlemen," he began. "Gentlemen," he repeated when silence fell upon the room, "If I could to take a quick moment to say one more thing and conduct one more bit of ship's business. Going into battle with a single lieutenant on a ship the size of our dear <u>Lawrence</u> would act as an undue burden on order, discipline, and the crew itself, so I have made a decision. This young man," he said, pointing to Dulaney, "will not go by Midshipman tomorrow. Instead, you will call him Lieutenant Forrest."

"Thank you, sir," said an embarrassed Dulaney to a torrent of applause and congratulations from everyone at the table.

"Now," continued Perry with one hand extended trying to quiet the table. "Now, it should go without saying that Mr. Forrest is one of the finest junior officers I have ever had the pleasure to command or work with. His knowledge and dedication to the marine and naval ways of life are rarely matched, and I am sure that he will lead the gundeck tomorrow with a sure hand."

The table broke out in hearty applause and cheers of "Hear, hear!" from Taylor and Breese.

"Is there any more business?" asked Perry. "No? Then dismissed."

With that the dinner ended, the attendees continued to congratulate Dulaney as they made their way to the upper deck to take in the autumn evening. The Commodore and Alexander stayed behind, sitting next to each other as the cook's mate cleared the final remnant of their meal. The young mate was an experienced hand and had cleaned the table before Mr. Brooks, who was the last to leave, saluted and walked out of the cabin.

"How now, Alex?" asked Perry dropping his brother's title but keeping the formal tone when they were finally alone. "What do you think of tomorrow's action?"

"I'm not sure." He said thinking of his inexperience.

"You've been in a couple of scrapes before," replied Perry, seemingly reading Alexander's thoughts.

"I can't imagine that they were be anything like tomorrow will be."

Perry smiled at his little brother, placed a kind hand on his head, and said, "You're a smart lad."

"Thank you, Oliver." He brushed his brother's hand from his head and fixed his hair. "Have you heard anything from father?"

"No," said Perry, his eyes brightening slightly, "but I *did* receive a letter from mother a few days ago. There was a bit addressed to you."

Alexander's heart raced. He hadn't heard from either of his parents in weeks. Perry stood up, walked to his desk, and rummaged through his papers until he had found the letter. He handed the water stained paper to Alexander and sat back down, picking up the spaniel and resting it in his lap.

"You can read through it all if you like," said the older brother, "but the part specifically for you is on the back of the third page."

Without a word, Alexander flipped back to his mother's message to him and hungrily ate up her words.

> Dearest Alex,
>
> Your brother has told me of your growth as a naval man, and his reports fill both your father and me with such pride. He says that you are destined to captain your own ship one day, and that he expects it to happen faster than it did even for him. Your dedication, determination, and dexterity will serve you well when you finally engage with the enemy. Nathaniel continues to look up to you and is following your career as closely as that of Oliver. You are quite the inspiration to your friends who have stayed behind as well
>
> As your mother, though, I must caution you to be prudent in your conduct. I would be immeasurably proud for any sacrifice you made for your country, but I would sooner have you

safely home, covered in marshal glory, than lost to sea because of the British guns and your own foolishness.

Alexander read the note twice before folding the paper and handing it back to his brother. "Do you really think that I could become a captain?" he asked.

"Of course," replied Oliver, taking the letter back. "You know that I could never lie to Mother. She can see through deception far too easily for that."

Alexander could see Oliver's tri-corner captain's hat on his desk. He imagined himself donning it as he led a ship full of men into battle. He imagined the fights with his country's enemies that would mark his ever-upward career, culminating in an admiralship. It was a glorious thought that made his heart race.

"Don't let it go to your head though, Alex," said Oliver, looking at his little brother with a hint of concern and bemusement at once. "You still have a few years of service before anyone will give you a ship."

"Wh...I know that," replied Alexander, slightly embarrassed., looking down at his hands.

"Are you sure? It almost looked like you were going to wrest command from me and lead us into battle tomorrow," teased Oliver. "I *did* want to talk to you about what to expect," he continued, dropping the playful tone. "I don't think Mother will ever forgive me if something happens to you."

"But, she said..." began Alexander.

"I know, I know. I read it too, but I know her better than you do. She'll understand and be proud of you, but she won't be of me. However, I want you to know that this decision isn't based purely on fear of Mother, but mostly on duty and the needs of the ship."

Alexander became nervous, a knot suddenly tightening in his stomach. "What is it?"

"You won't have a gun crew tomorrow. You are a good officer, but battles need more than guns."

The younger Perry slouched in his chair. This was not what any midshipman wanted to hear, especially right after Dulaney's promotion. It felt unfair.

"Sit up, Mr. Perry," snapped the commodore. Alexander did so. "You've been on deck during drills, but I don't think you realize how chaotic battles can get. It becomes hard for anyone to hear you five feet away, even on deck, in the middle of the fighting, so you'll be my aide, my messenger. You'll need to keep your head low as you run back and forth, but you are the best for the job. You're the smallest person I can trust with this. You know the ship as well as anyone, you're faster than most, and your memory is good. Do you think you'll be able to do this for me?"

Alexander's trepidation and anger slowly melted away as his older brother continued to speak. He had been drilling on the guns for weeks, and he had been excited to test those skills in battle. And yet, he would have been confined to the gun deck, able to see no more of the battle than what he could gleam through the ever thickening gun smoke. As the commodore's aide, he would primarily be on the quarterdeck and able to see everything. He would carry orders to every part of the ship and witness the battle from every angle. Not even Oliver would see as much as Alexander would. His excitement bubbled up within him so much that he could hardly stay seated. He wanted to run and jump, but he kept calm, fighting the gleeful smile plastered across his face.

"Well, Mr. Perry?" asked the commodore. "I hope that you find your assigned duties to be acceptable."

"Yes, sir!" Alexander almost shouted. "I mean, I'll do my best, sir," he said more modestly.

"I expect no less," replied Perry. He stood. "Now come, let's join the rest on deck."

The senior officers had gathered together on the quarterdeck while the midshipmen hung about at the bottom of the steps. As the commodore and Alexander passed the junior officers, Perry insisted that they join him at the pilot's wheel to enjoy the evening together. On the quarterdeck they found that Mr. Brooks had dropped his aloofness from dinner and was leading the officers in a rendition of "Johnny Has Gone for a Soldier". He seemed more natural and at home out in the open air then in the cramped quarters below deck.

Lieutenant Brooks finished the song with its final verse ("She'll dye her dress, She'll dye it red, and through the streets she'll beg for bread, The lad that she loves from her has fled. Johnny has gone for a soldier.") and conversation steadily began again. Dulaney quizzed Alexander about his meeting with the commodore. Alexander explained his duties for the battle and found that the other midshipmen seemed more jealous of Alexander's new position than Dulaney's. Dulaney was more likely going to be in charge of the gun deck since he was the most junior lieutenant, and Henry, Augustus, and Peleg would probably be in charge of individual gun crews. All three would see the battle in a smoke filled dungeon with only tiny windows in the smoke for air.

While in the midst of their discussion on the merits of playing the role of aide to the commodore, the talk shifted to a general discussion about the war. Augustus had remained distant from the conversation. He was always at the conversation's edge as though he wanted to take part but didn't know how to involve himself or what to say.

"I'd heard that the <u>Cuba</u> was captured last year," said Peleg.

"Was it? By whom?" asked Dulaney.

"I'd heard it was the HMS <u>Devastation</u>," replied Peleg.

"The <u>De</u>..." started Augustus.

No one spoke for a moment. They waited to hear what Augustus had to say.

"My father had a friend," began Augustus wringing his hand, "Thomas Horton. He was born in Albany but moved to England when he was little and his father found work in Surrey. He didn't move back until his twenties and never lost his English accent." He paused again. "Thomas became the purser on a merchant ship and got impressed into service on a British vessel when a Royal captain heard him speak, declaring him a subject of the crown. We aren't sure what happened next, but we do know that he served on the <u>Devastation</u> for at least two months. We've heard a couple of different versions of the story, but most likely he tried to escape and they hung him. He was my brother's godfather."

Still, no one spoke as Augustus took a moment to collect himself.

"My brother joined the army the day we found out and my father convinced our congressman to secure my commission. I wanted to help. I know that I'm no more than a bumbler, but I've been trying."

Alexander put his hand on Augustus's shoulder and said, "We all know someone like that. I have a friend, John Dickenson, who's serving on a British vessel right now. He doesn't even have an accent, but his name is the same as a British deserter." Calling Dickenson a friend was a stretch, more like an acquaintance on the water, but Alexander wanted to help Augustus feel less alone.

The other officers shared their own stories of British injustice on the sea, and it quickly became apparent that Augustus felt more like a member of the family than ever before.

Seven bells had rung some time before, so the junior officers saluted their captain and made their way below deck to prepare for the night's rest. The midshipmen refused to look at one another below deck, somewhat terrified by the idea of being responsible for the lives of each other as the thought of battle came back to them and they unpacked their hammocks, hanging them from the ceiling. Before they had finished, the deep and sonorous voice of the boatswain called out, "Stand by your hammocks," from above deck.

Afraid that he would be unable to sleep, Alexander slowly climbed into his cloth bed (socks firmly on his feet) unable to control his chattering knees. But he soon found himself dozing off as Dulaney hummed some old ditty.

CHAPTER IV: March Over Water

The Brig Niagara by Lance Woodworth

Alexander had learned to sleep deeply long ago (a useful measure for jostling nights at sea), but he was on edge that early morning. Something told him the night before had been no dream, the orders no fantasy, and that they would sail into battle that day.

"Sail, ho!" Alexander was sure a voice, muffled by a hundred feet and several layers of wooden deck above, had said.

"Where away?" came Dulaney's voice, much closer and louder. He had been on deck since four o'clock as officer of the watch.

"To the northward and westward, from the River."

There couldn't have been many sailing vessels on the lake those days, but the fact that the sails were coming from the northwest told what Alexander that it was the enemy. The only question now was whether they had come in force to fight or were on some scouting mission. It all depended on that new flagship of theirs, the Detroit.

Before the brief exchange between Dulaney and the watchman had even finished, Alexander bounded from his hammock, clumsily yet speedily bundled it into his storage space, bolted from the cabin, and jumped up two flights of stairs to the quarterdeck. He couldn't feel the fatigue on his eyes or even the heavy thumping of his heart. He couldn't hear the murmurs of the seamen or the calling of the morning birds. All he could see was the tree line on the northern edge of Put-in-Bay. All he could hear was the water lazily slapping the sides of the <u>Lawrence</u>. All he could feel was the worryingly soft breeze.

Lieutenant Yarnall came up on deck, his uniform in perfect order and his hat affixed atop his head like a statue of General Washington. He greeted Dulaney while returning the salutes of the midshipmen, all of whom gathered by Alexander at the taffrail and were trying to see past the tree-line into the lake itself.

"Report, Mr. Forrest," said Yarnall calmly and professionally.

"Sails spotted nor-western, sir. About fifteen miles," replied Dulaney in kind.

"Excellent. Prepare to make sail."

It was such a simple order delivered so plainly that had Alexander, along with the entire crew, not been through the exercises dozens of times over the last few weeks the managed chaos that erupted after would have been shocking. The motions and orders and changes came so naturally that it was as though the crew had been born capturing the wind. The feat was all the more impressive considering those Kentucky backwoodsmen had come onboard having operated no more than row boats on small streams. Yet now, on the morning of an engagement, they operated so proficiently with the sails, the anchor, and the general storage of unneeded items that they could match, and needed to rival, the British navy's own reputation for efficiency.

The wind was lightly blowing from the south-southwest, which wanted to push the ships north-northeast, directly into the peninsula that created Put-in-Bay. Any sailor worth have his salt knew how to use a basic sail to push a ship in almost any direction. Alexander recited the orders in his head before either Yarnall or Forrest shouted them. Navigating southeast to maneuver out of the bay was no easy task, but pushing northwest towards the enemy was going to be even harder. On top of that the British fleet had the weather gage, and, with that advantage, would be able to dictate how the upcoming battle would begin.

"Mr. Perry," said Yarnall between other orders.

"Aye, sir" replied Alexander, saluting, and fighting the sudden rush of excitement.

"Report to the captain, if you please."

"Aye, sir," replied Alexander with a quick salute. He nodded to Dulaney, who nodded back, and ran down the stairs to the main deck and the captain's quarters. He had lost himself a bit in the excitement but managed to steady his nerves when he appeared before Commodore Perry. Alexander tried to think of nothing but doing his duty, with limited success.

"Mr. Perry," said the Commodore as he put his jacket on, looking out the ship's rear window, "do you have a report?"

"Aye, sir. The enemy has been sighted to the north-northwest, and we are currently making sail to meet him," replied Alexander almost surprised at himself for being able to get out the entire sentence.

"Thank you, Mr. Perry," replied the Commodore. He secured the strap of his boot, petted the dog, and walked up to the midshipman. The older Perry paused by his brother, looked up for a second to ensure that they were alone, placed his hand on Alexander's shoulder, and said, "You'll be fine, Alex. Be strong."

Alexander's mind, which had been racing between images of the upcoming battle and home quieted with his older brother's embrace. Alexander looked up at the caring brown eyes of his captain and sibling. Even in those dim quarters, lit only by the morning sun, Alexander could see the same eyes of their mother who had lovingly raised them and filled them with the fervor for the sea. In that moment, in that strange wilderness, and in the bowels of that new warship, Alexander felt like he was at home.

The illusion faded as Commodore Perry said, "Are you ready, Mr. Perry?"

"Aye, sir," replied Midshipman Perry with a salute, control continuing to hold over his voice.

"Very good. Now, to the quarterdeck, young man," said the Commodore, returning the young officer's salute. "I'll be right behind you."

Alexander left the captain's cabin and ran across the main deck, weaving through the hectic motion of the dozens of bodies that fluttered around the ship getting it ready to sail.

"Oi! Mr. Perry!" came a shout. It was Henry Laub straddling the stairs from the gundeck on the opposite side of the ship. He waved Alexander over so he didn't need to shout. "Is the big one in the water? Are we going to fight?"

"I don't know yet," Alexander replied with a quick wave as he ran up the steps to the quarterdeck, but Henry's instinct was right. If the British left the <u>Detroit</u> at port, the enemy probably wouldn't fight, especially with the entire American squadron out in force.

Gaining the quarterdeck, Alexander found the newly promoted Second Lieutenant Forrest monitoring the extending of the sails and First Lieutenant Yarnall going over the depth chart of Put-in-Bay with the pilot, Mr. Steers, as he held the wheel.

"This is the hard part, Mr. Steers. Five points starboard for a hundred yards and then a ten point turn to larboard, please."

"Aye, sir."

Commodore Perry, his hat fixed securely on his head and his uniform, complete with shiny brass buttons and a creaseless jacket, handsomely composed, arrived on the quarterdeck with every sailor saluting him as he passed. Alexander could see, if only for a brief moment, the awe and respect each man held for his commanding officer in their faces. Alexander could imagine the men offering to throw themselves into the cannons once their shot ran out in order to guarantee their commodore's victory.

"Good morning, John," said the Commodore when he returned Lieutenant Yarnall's salute. "How many sails?"

"We count four ships so far, sir."

Commodore Perry took the chart from Lieutenant Yarnall and made a mark with his pencil near their position. "What do you think? Are the rest hidden by the horizon?"

"I don't think so, sir. They're only nine miles distant."

"So they're behind the ones we can see, then."

"Unless they've fallen at least three miles behind."

"We could only be so lucky," said Perry with a smile.

"Yes, sir. If only," replied Yarnell, his face as stoic as ever.

"Nine miles...what position?"

"North-northwest, sir."

"That would put them about...here," said Perry lightly marking a spot on the map with his pencil. "In which direction are they sailing?"

"Westward, sir."

"Once we're out of the bay see if you can get us here." Perry placed the chart down and pointed to a spot about two miles east of the enemy's position.

"It won't be easy with this wind, sir."

"Do what you can, John. I want the weather gage, and if God won't give it to me, then I think I may need to take it."

"But sir, that won't..."

"Trust me, John."

"Aye, sir."

"Oh, and is she out there?" asked Perry, referring to the <u>Detroit</u>.

"Aye, sir. She is."

"Good, I didn't want to get everyone excited for nothing."

They soon found themselves out of the bay and in open water. The flagship came out first and the rest followed in their pre-determined order of battle: the <u>Caledonia</u> followed by the <u>Niagara</u>, <u>Somers</u>, <u>Porcupine</u>, <u>Tigress</u>, <u>Trippe</u>, <u>Scorpion</u>, and the <u>Ariel</u>. Few signals were necessary: just enough to tell those following the <u>Lawrence</u> what direction to take and how much sail to use. The British fleet maintained its westward heading, the wind still blew north-northeast, and Perry wanted the American fleet to sail northwest which required fighting the wind. They couldn't head straight since the wind would actually push them backwards. Instead, the fleet tacked back and forth, swinging around the desired direction allowing for slow progress. It was a tactic that Alexander had long been familiar with. He had used it many times in small skiffs as he had sailed around the islands near Newport. It was a bit trying on his own, but much easier on any one person as part of a crew of more than one hundred.

"Tell me, John," said the Commodore after the first few maneuvers, which took about an hour. "On what heading is the enemy?"

"Still westward, sir."

Perry fell silent for a moment. Alexander knew that face: the slightly aloof sternness of the Commodore's brows that his brother made every time he calculated something in his head.

"More than enough time for a lesson. If you please, gather the junior officers."

"Aye, sir," replied the lieutenant. "Mr. Perry," he said to Alexander, "please retrieve Mr. Laub, Mr. Swartwout, and Mr. Denham to the quarterdeck."

"Aye, sir," replied Alexander. With a quick salute he was off to the gundeck bounding down past sailors, diligently busy preparing the guns. Hardly any of them noticed the quiet steps of the midshipman, but Schroeder, one of the Newport men on Alexander's gun crew waved at the young officer as he passed.

On the main deck, preparations were well on their way. The guns were in place, shot had been distributed, and the powder was being passed out. Henry was directing the action while Augustus and Peleg were concentrating on their own individual crews.

"Commodore wants us on deck, Mr. Laub," said Alexander as he approached Henry.

"What…," began Henry before noticing a sailor out of the corner of his eye. "Oi! Don't overload the cannons! How many times do I have to tell you? What does he want us for?" he asked Alexander.

"He seems to think that we're due a lesson."

"Well, how long do we have until we're in range?"

"We're still miles off."

"What's going on?" asked Augustus who had left his crew to manage themselves.

"Commodore wants us on deck for lessons."

"Seems an odd time for it," opined Peleg who had joined the trio.

"Maybe, but are you going to tell him no?" asked Alexander.

"I guess not," said Henry. "Mr. Lauren, please oversee the rest of the preparations."

"Aye, sir," replied the gunner's mate.

All five midshipmen were soon on the quarterdeck. Actually, Alexander corrected himself, it was only four now. Dulaney was a second lieutenant and not a midshipman anymore. Nevertheless, none of the junior officers could concentrate on anything but the promised action. It was excitement and dread mixed together in a combination that both pinched their stomachs and caused their hands to tremble. Alexander, for his part, did his best to listen to the Commodore. It usually wasn't a problem to absorb the lessons from the soothing voice and warm eyes of their commanding officer, but today was no usual day.

"Who can explain the order of battle to me?" asked the Commodore. "Why is the <u>Lawrence</u> out first?"

No one responded. Alexander's eyes drifted to where he imagined the British to be to the Northwest.

"Oh come now. I would expect two answers: one easy and one more difficult. Can anyone give me the easy reason?"

"It's to even out the guns, sir," said Henry.

"Very good, but please explain."

Henry shuffled about for a second before he responded. "It is in the interests of both sides that the ships with the most guns should go up against one another or else each side would yield their gun advantage and let them loose upon smaller ships. The smaller vessels would do little to no damage to the larger ones while suffering terrible damage themselves." Alexander thought of the <u>Detroit</u>. It had twenty guns to the <u>Lawrence</u>'s eighteen. That two-gun difference suddenly felt very large.

"Very good, Mr. Laub. Now, can anyone give me the more difficult answer?"

None of them spoke.

"Have none of you read <u>The Art of War at Sea</u> by Oliveira?"

They all shook their heads. None had.

"My copy is in the family library. John, did you happen to bring a copy with you?"

"No, sir. I only read Captain Evan's copy while on the <u>Chesapeake</u>."

"That's too bad. We'll have to make it a priority when we make port again. It is no matter for the moment, though.

The Commodore explained how it was the Portuguese that had first developed the idea formally while Oliveira, of Portuguese descent himself, proved the idea's genius and utility by comparing a fleet in line to the battlements of a castle. He went on to explain the difficulties of keeping a fleet of ships, all with different sails and keels, to maintain the requisite distance and prevent any holes in the formation. Maintaining a line tended to slow the fastest vessels to the speed of the slowest. Alexander thought of how the slower sloops would have the same difficultly keeping up with the double masted brigs while beginning to wonder, and even worry, that they might not be able to maintain formation. He tried to bring up the topic of breaking the line, but the Commodore brushed of the suggestion saying that the maneuver was so rare and difficult that the basic summary from the night before should we enough the time being.

As the lesson continued with examples from the Napoleonic War, the <u>Lawrence</u> struggled to endure the unfavorable wind. Every half hour or so the ship tacked ninety degrees left and then right, taking its bow across the wind trying to build any momentum across the water and into battle. By ten o'clock, the squadron had only advanced about a mile from the bay, while the British continued their lazy sail westward.

With the lesson at an end, the other three midshipmen returned to the gundeck while Alexander accompanied the Commodore to the pilot's station where Lieutenant Yarnall and the Mr. Steers struggled to force the wind to Perry's will.

"What's the good word, John?" asked the Commodore lightly as though he were asking after the weather at port.

"I can't find one, sir," replied the lieutenant. "It'll take all day to get into the right position, and the enemy will be able to pick us apart whenever they choose."

The commodore peered out over the water in the direction of the British squadron. They were still too far away to see from the deck, the curve of the Earth's surface continued to hide the enemy from everyone on board save those high up in the rigging and crow's nest. And yet, looking out over the pristine and still blue lake, Alexander could almost feel the enemy's presence.

"Very well, John. Bring us…"

At that moment, Providence smiled upon the American fleet. The wind, which had so easily and obstinately frustrated the Commodore's plans, shifted suddenly. The breeze, which had been blowing steadily from the west southwest turned and blew from the southeast, directly at the Lawrence's back.

"Commodore…" began Yarnall, interrupting his commanding officer.

"I see it, John," replied the commodore who regarded the suddenly billowing sails and the happily flapping flags and pendants that bent to the northwest. "We have them now. Send the order. Northwest. Straight at 'em." With the wind having changed, they no longer needed to find their advantage. Nature's God had given it to them.

"Aye, sir!" exclaimed Yarnall with a broad smile suddenly on his face, replacing the stoic and nearly sad look he so frequently bore.

The news spread across the ship like a blaze, and the heat and exhaustion of several hours of hard work was forgotten as a frenzied thrill replaced it. Soon, Hannibal Collins broke out into a song and had the crew singing along with him in short order.

> Hail Columbia, happy land!
> Hail, ye heroes, heav'n-born band,
> Who fought and bled in freedom's cause,
> Who fought and bled in freedom's cause,
> And when the storm of war was gone
> Enjoy'd the peace your valor won.
> Let independence be our boast,
> Ever mindful what it cost;
> Ever grateful for the prize,
> Let its altar reach the skies.

The patriotic song spread out over the waves, and Alexander could hear the crew of the Caledonia behind them pick up the anthem. They were headed into battle for the glory of their country against the enemy of liberty with the weather gage and the advantage. It was hard to not get swept up in the emotion of the moment. In front of the senior officers, and especially the commodore, Alexander tried to remain composed, but as soon as Commodore Perry joined into the second verse, all pretense melted away and Alexander joined in.

As the song died down, regular order regained its grip on the whole crew who continued the work of readying the ship for battle. Perry walked up to Yarnall and asked, "Do we have their order of battle yet?"

"Aye, sir," replied Yarnall who handed his commander a slip of paper.

"The Chippewa is in front of the Detroit?"

"It looks that way, sir."

"Very well. A small change and we should be ready. If you can, please signal Captain Elliott to let the Caledonia fall behind him."

Alexander ran the order to Henry who was in charge of signals. Seconds later a seaman had raised the blue pennant to the foresail. The Caledonia almost instantly made to slow by drawing up its sails and pulled to port to allow the Niagara to pass.

As the two ships came along each other behind the Lawrence, Commodore Perry, from the aft of his flagship, waved to Captain Elliott.

"The little schooner is out in front, sir!" cried Elliott through a speaking trumpet over the sloshing water.

"That she is, Captain," replied Perry with his own megaphone. "Please come up behind us, and we'll face the Detroit together."

Elliott didn't respond for a moment as he turned his gaze northward and the still empty horizon. It was any man's guess what passed through the decorated captain's head in that moment.

"Captain?" called Perry.

"I beg your pardon, sir. Of course, sir."

The conversation ended and the Niagara made it fully past the Caledonia to fall in behind the Lawrence.

"Mr. Perry," said the commodore to his aide. "Please retrieve my battle flag from my cabin. It's time to show the crew."

Alexander's heart was racing and he couldn't remember the journey from the quarterdeck to the cabin, but everything seemed to stop when he saw the blue folds of fabric in the dim late morning light. Amongst the captain's things on his desk, Yarnall had folded the flag so that one of the pristine white letters peaked out from an edge. Alexander guessed that it was the "T" and found that he couldn't bring himself to touch it. It was almost as though the flag were a holy relic of some great saint, and his fingers would defile the sacred fabric. "Don't give up the ship," Alexander whispered to himself as he ran his fingers along the material before finally picking it up, tucking it beneath his open vest, and walking back into the sun.

Commodore Perry thanked Alexander when the midshipman gained the quarterdeck and asked for him and Lieutenant Forrest to hold opposite ends of the banner open for the crew to see.

Perry interrupted a slight but tepid murmur the crew when he spoke out to the men of the <u>Lawrence</u>.

"My brothers in arms! Look out there!" The commodore pointed before them. "Can you see the enemy?"

Alexander peered out with the rest of them and made out the line of sales that was just then peeking out from the horizon. He could make out four distinct shapes. Two more must have been hidden either by an already visible ship or the horizon itself. Alexander realized that through the morning part of him hadn't believed it, as though the intelligence had been lies and the men in the bird's nest had mistaken the wings of gulls for sails. But there it was: tangible proof. Today they would meet the enemy.

"Now this flag," continued Perry after Alexander and Dulaney had unfurled it. "What does it say?"

There was a momentary silence until one of the crew, Hoffman from South Carolina, called out, "Don't give up the ship!"

"I would never do any such thing, would you?" replied Perry.

"No!" shouted back Hoffman as the rest of the crew both laughed and said the same thing.

"My brave lads, the inscription on this flag…these words are the last words of the gallant Captain Lawrence after whom this vessel is named. "Don't give up the ship!" Shall I hoist it?"

"Aye, yie, sir!" they all shouted together.

Filled with youthful excitement and impatience for glory, Alexander helped the commodore attach the flag to the mainmast and hoist it above the pregnant sails. All eyes followed its ascent. The navy flag stood out from the sapphire sky, flapping vigorously in the wind, pointing forward as to direct the whole fleet to its quarry before them. The men cheered again. Alexander followed the commodore through the throng as he began his pre-battle inspection and ordered the midday grog passed out. He spoke to, not only the officers, but every man, even if only to give some small word of encouragement.

"We'll be at 'em soon. Then you can show them the kind of stuff that make an American sailor," he said to the Kentucky men.

"Your father would be proud," he said to a Newport man.

"Don't be afraid, seaman. As soon as we get close enough, we'll make it clear that America is now at least Britain's equal."

On the gundeck, Commodore Perry looked over every gun and demanded demonstrations of as much functionality short of actually firing the weapons as possible. He came to Peleg's crew and began his inspection like the others.

"Any issues, Mr. Denham?"

"No, sir…except…" hesitatingly replied the midshipman.

"Out with it, son. I'd rather find out about it now than in the middle of battle."

"Well, sir, she won't rise about thirty degrees. We won't be able to aim for the enemy's sails, sir."

Without another word, the commodore was on his knees, inspecting the cannon's carriage. After a moment, he motioned for his aide to join him.

"Can you figure it out, Mr. Perry?" asked the commanding officer as he wrapped an arm around the midshipman's shoulders and pointed to the carriage.

Alexander pushed in closer, squeezing into position, and trying to bring his head around wood and metal to find anything wrong. It only took a few seconds to see the damage to the mount. "I think, sir, that we'd need to replace the screw."

The brothers remained crouched next to each other as though intimates sharing a secret.

"Well, what do you think, Mr. Perry? What should we do now? Do we have to fix the carriage?"

Alexander tried to think it through. Their guns had smaller barrels and were best for shorter distances which meant it was more important for the American fleet to be able to direct fire up or down trying to take out the enemy's sails or sinking her with directed shots. A gun that couldn't shoot up was of limited use, but if the line of battle held then moving the cannon from the starboard to the port side could replace a malfunctioning gun with a perfectly sound one without risking much. He told the commodore his idea and reasons.

Perry smiled and said, "Very good, Alex. What do you think? Is there enough time to move the guns?"

Alexander looked blankly at his brother for a moment, unable to remember how much longer they had until they were in range of the enemy. Oliver must have seen the small panic in his brother's eyes and nodded to the open air above the taffrail. Alexander quickly jutted his head up to gauge the distance to the enemy. They had at least an hour until they were in range of the enemy's guns and probably between a quarter and half hour more until the American's could return fire with any efficacy. With solid information and a conclusion, Alexander returned to his brother and said, "There should be enough time."

"Good, then let Lieutenant Forrest know that it's my order, Mr. Perry."

"Yes, sir," Alexander replied with a smile.

As Alexander explained to Dulaney, Commodore Perry continued his inspection, combining his critical and exacting eye with his upbeat demeanor. Alexander watched the new lieutenant organize and complete the task (removing the gun on the port side, moving the starboard gun to the newly vacant hole, and replacing the port gun on the starboard side) and reported back to the commodore who had finished his inspection and was giving some final words of encouragement to the officers of the gundeck.

Soon they were atop the quarterdeck. The ship was finally ready for battle and a nervous quiet had settled over the crew. Even Hannibal Collins couldn't find his voice for a song.

"Report, John," said the commodore to his lieutenant.

"We're about two miles distant from the <u>Lady Prevost</u> and <u>Little Belt</u>. We'll be in range of the <u>Detroit</u>'s guns momentarily."

"Very good. What's your feel of the men?"

"They're ready sir. Nervous, but they'll do their jobs."

"They'll do well," replied Perry, agreeing with his subordinate. He smiled like a father.

The quarterdeck fell silent as every officer and crewman peered out at the billowing sails that become more and more imposing with every passing moment. It was a sight of beauty. The pristine white sails that billowed with the full wind, the clean blue water that surrounded them with the perfect azure sky above and the distant green line of trees that marked the horizon. If Alexander had been a painter instead of a sailor he would have made this vista his next subject. Just replace the Union Jacks with the 15 stars and 15 stripes of the American flag, and it could rest in any great home or public building in the country. Instead, Alexander knew that the idyllic view would soon shatter in fire, smoke, and blood. It was beautiful, but temporary.

Commodore Perry slowly stepped towards the railing and indicated that his aide should follow him. Perry rested his hands flat against the wood, idly rubbing the grain with his thumb as they looked at the closing enemy.

"I've been thinking, Alex," Oliver said to his brother in a whisper. "I've been thinking that when I'm old, fat, and useless, I'll probably fill my last days by writing a book of my life, and I wonder what I'll write about today."

"We'll win, won't we?"

"Oh, it's not that." He paused before he continued. "But will I be able to say that I fought or ran? That I met the enemy bravely? That I made my country proud not just with, perhaps not even with, a favorable result, but with at least my comportment in achieving it?" The two brothers made eye contact for a moment before looking back out to the enemy fleet which seemed to both be closer than ever and eternally out of reach at the same time. "Will I meet today bravely?"

"You are the bravest man I know, Oliver."

"You've never been in battle, little brother. The explosions of cannons, the crack of musket fire, and the swing of swords: it changes men, even the brave ones."

"But *you've* been in battle, and you fought bravely."

"To be honest, I hardly remember those fights, and I don't know how I was able to stand up on deck as my friends and brothers fell down beside me." Oliver looked at his brother and saw doubt and fear in his eyes. "I may not know how, but I do know that if even I could find the courage then so can you. We are both sons to the same unyielding father and strong mother. I don't know if it helped me before, but I was always able to concentrate on my duties while under fire. Don't think of America, President Madison, or George Washington. Don't even think of Mother and Father. Just think of your duty to this ship and your brothers on it. We are a new nation, Alex. Help me prove our place."

As the commodore finished, a bugle sounded form the <u>Detroit</u> in the distance. Both men stood up straight, and the enemy released its first shot at the <u>Lawrence</u>.

The battle had begun.

CHAPTER V: The Battle Begins

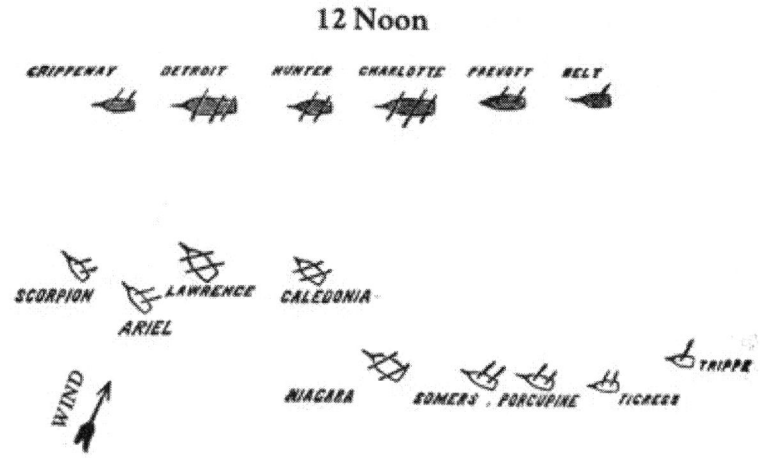

"12 Noon" from *The Naval War of 1812* by Theodore Roosevelt

Before the explosion of the distant gun had faded, the ball fell a few hundred feet short of the <u>Lawrence</u> with a dull splash and a hollow thump. As calm briefly returned to the still lake, the hearty voices of the British sailors carried over the mile and a half that separated the American flagship and the <u>Detroit</u>, singing:

> Rule Britannia!
> Britannia rule the waves
> Britons never, never, never shall be slaves.

Hannibal Collins began an enthusiastic rendition of "Yankee Doodle Dandy" which most of the crew began to join when the <u>Detroit</u> fired its second shot, clipping the railing on the American brig's deck, sending wooden shards across the ship and harmlessly into the water. The impact sounded worse than it was, but it still chilled the mood on deck and focused the crew back to their task at hand.

"Mr. Perry," said the commodore amid the rising cacophony of British guns that were becoming hard to see behind a thick and growing cloud of smoke.

Alexander reported to Perry with a salute. "Aye, sir?"

"Report on the fleet, if you please."

"Aye, yie, sir."

Alexander ran aft, his heart racing, and found Dulaney with his gun crew. Their guns were quiet, cool, and unfired even under the swelling barrage of cannon shot, the American guns lacking any effectiveness for at least another three quarters of a mile. The two friends exchanged a knowing glance before returning to their duties.

"Where's the rest of the fleet?" asked Alexander incredulously as he looked to aft and saw much more of the blue lake and sapphire sky than he had expected, a sickening feeling suddenly rising in his stomach. The Caledonia sailed behind them and the Scorpion and Ariel to windward on the port quarter of the Lawrence, but the other five ships were out of position. The battle hadn't really begun yet, and already things were falling apart. "What's Elliott doing?" he asked referring to the captain of the Niagara which had continued on its original course westward instead of following the Lawrence to the northwest and into close action. "Doesn't he see the signal?"

"Is the signal up?" asked Dulaney. "Can he see it?"

Alexander point to the navy flag with the last words of Captain Lawrence flapping in the breeze. "They can see it in Pennsylvania," Alexander replied almost angrily.

"He's not going to hang back and just use his long guns, is he?" asked Dulaney in between a pair of orders to his gun crew.

It didn't matter. All Alexander could do was gather information and let the commodore decide on any action. "Where are the others?"

"There," Dulaney pointed at the tiny sails two miles back. "I don't think they can catch the wind enough to keep up."

Alexander leaned over the rail and squinted into the distance. He thought he saw some movement at the sides of the closest schooner that looked like sweeps propelling the ship forward. Their doubled efforts did little to save him from the sinking feeling in his gut.

"At least they're trying," said Dulaney sardonically.

Without another word, Alexander bolted back to his commanding officer and reported what he had seen, doing his best to maintain his professionalism.

Commodore Perry had been calmly studying the enemy's formation which was as tight and professionally executed as one would expect from the British navy. He seemed unflappable even as the enemy's guns continued to fire and the first casualties fell on the American deck. That steadiness, however, momentarily weakened when his young aide informed him of the <u>Niagara</u>'s position. It was only a brief second, but Alexander saw his brother's eyes widen in panic before returning to normal as he replied, "Very good." Perry pulled his pocket watch from his waistcoat, noticed the time, and said, "John, order the fleet to open fire, if you please."

"Aye, sir," Yarnall replied as he marched to the young bugler. After a quick exchange the young seaman took the brass instrument to his lips and played the attack order. Within seconds, the din of battle grew ever louder as the nearby <u>Scorpion</u> and <u>Ariel</u> fired past the <u>Lawrence</u> and into the enemy's line, their shots having little effect when they did manage a hit.

"Fire the longs, John," ordered the commodore. They were still too far from the enemy for the majority of their guns to have any effect. Their two long twelve-pounders were the only guns on deck that could cause any damage, much less reach, the <u>Detroit</u>, which still sailed about a mile away. "Take us within half-pistol shot," the commodore ordered his first lieutenant.

Yarnall stood with the pilot and helped steady the nervous sailor. As the ships came closer and closer, the mighty guns on the <u>Detroit</u> and the <u>Lady Prevost</u> continued to pummel the <u>Lawrence</u>, injuring over a dozen men before the American vessel could bear up and present its starboard broadside to the enemy. Alexander watched Kentuckians he hardly knew and Newport men he had known his whole life fall to canister, ball, and grapeshot. Those that could manage to continue fighting despite their wounds soldiered on; the rest resigned themselves to going to the surgeon below deck professing to return as soon as they could. Even those men obviously near death swore to rejoin their mates and fight to the last.

"I think we have it, sir!" shouted Mr. Steers as he pulled the wheel leftward, showing the <u>Lawrence</u>'s broadside to the <u>Detroit</u>.

"No!" shouted Yarnall.

The two ships were about five hundred yards apart, which was still too far for the American carronades to cause any kind of serious damage.

"What's going on, John?"

"We've presented too early, sir. We'll need to bear away again to regain the weather gage."

Steadily, the <u>Lawrence</u> continued her turn, exposing her aft to the enemy. In that moment, the enemy's fire increased as they began to aim for the American's steering.

"Make it quick, John. We won't survive for long like this."

"Aye, sir."

The aft of a ship is narrower than its sides, so while taking out the steering can nearly cripple a ship, it is also harder to hit, especially when the enemy's broadside is not directly pointed at the target and it can move away with decent speed. Both of those conditions marked the Lawrence's turn which helped save it from any catastrophic damage to its aft. Cannon balls whizzed by the brig harmlessly and splashed into the water before the bow. Grapeshot tore holes in the sails and canisters thudded against the wooden hull without breaking through. Amidst it all, the commodore stood tall, issuing orders and acting as a stalwart symbol as the Lawrence's crew looked to him for strength in the chaos.

At about a thousand yards, Perry turned to his first lieutenant and said, "I think that's good enough, John. Bring us back around."

"Aye, sir. Starboard, ninety degrees, Mr. Steers," said Yarnall.

"Aye, sir," replied the pilot.

Lieutenant Brooks joined the crowd around the wheel with his customary smile on his face. He put his hand on Alexander's shoulder, winked at the junior officer, and turned to Commodore Perry.

"Something tells me that move wasn't planned, sir."

Perry looked past the marine to the Detroit hidden behind the billowing smoke from her guns which continued their destructive fire, becoming only more so with every closing yard.

"It was only a hiccup. We'll take them yet," replied Perry with a smile.

"Wonderful to hear, Commodore! Should I have the marines prepare to board the enemy, sir?"

"Not just yet, Lieutenant. Let's see how the day evolves first, shall we? Mr. Perry," said the commodore to Alexander, switching to his calm and commanding air, "distance to the enemy, if you please."

The commodore could tell the distance between two objects on calm waters better than anyone else on the ship. It was a test, not just of Alexander's eyes, but of his nerves at this early stage of battle. The midshipman took a step forward and squinted through the smoke.

"Four hundred yards and closing, sir."

"Very good. Mr. Steers, begin to bring us to larboard. I wish to give the British a warm greeting from America, if you please."

"Aye, sir!"

"I still want us at half-pistol shot, though, Mr. Steers, so don't take us too far out."

"Aye, sir," replied the helmsman, embarrassment sneaking into his voice.

The Lawrence began to veer to the left, and the Detroit began to come into view of the starboard carronades. The ships were still too far apart for the American guns to be terribly effective, but at least they could begin to put a fight.

As the crew saw their target getting closer and closer, the air became more and more tense. Their inactivity and helplessness in the face of the terrible British onslaught was coming to an end. Soon the Americans would be able to show through actions what they had only been able to express in words. All of their anger at the unjust deeds the British had taken against their American brothers at sea, all of their rage at the massacres of their countrymen at the hands of the enemy, and all of their fury at the impudence the enemy's king had shown the American people would now be articulated with fire and metal. They were there to protect their nation against an invader, and they would repel those intruders all of the three thousand miles back to England. It was here that these proud Americans would demonstrate their country's worth and proper place in the pantheon of nations. They were no longer a group of fledgling colonies, but a union of states worthy of respect and deference.

"How far are we now, Mr. Perry?"

"About three hundred yards, sir."

"Very good. Fire at will, John." Alexander marveled at the composure in his brother's voice while giving the order to open battle with a British squadron. The commodore seemed to be trying to hide a small smile.

"Aye, sir!" replied Yarnall before he turned to the open deck below. "Fire all!" he shouted over the sounds of the British guns. The order jumped down the line as the head of every gun crew took up the call, ending with Dulaney at the aft, but Alexander couldn't hear any of them as the American guns joined the discord of battle. All of a sudden, Alexander couldn't catch what anyone was saying more than six inches away. The world had become a place of smoke, thunder, and metal tearing through wood and flesh alike. The quick moments between explosions were filled with the screams of the wounded or the broken shouting of seamen and officers equally struggling to be heard in the pandemonium.

It was a testament to the commodore's leadership and skills as a drillmaster that the deck of the Lawrence did not descend into pure anarchy. Men were more likely to remain at their stations loading and firing guns than even notice their injuries much less abandon their posts in search of medical aid from Dr. Parsons below deck.

Sailing Master Taylor approached the commodore, saluted, and leaned forward to shout into his ear. Eager for any more information on the battle around them, Alexander stretched to eavesdrop. It was difficult in the heat of battle, but the midshipman managed to hear most of the conversation.

"Sir! The <u>Queen Charlotte</u> has turned her guns on us!" shouted Taylor, pointing to the sixteen-gun sloop.

"Where is the <u>Niagara</u>?"

"She won't come to close action, sir!" The sailing master pointed to the south-east at the solitary brig that expelled the occasional puff of smoke from their pair of long twelves. "Did you give Captain Elliott orders to stay back?"

Perry did not respond to Mr. Taylor's question. Instead, he pointed to the three-gun <u>Caledonia</u> which had taken up the <u>Niagara</u>'s position and was giving everything it could to both the <u>Queen Charlotte</u> and the <u>Lady Prevost</u>, despite the American ship's inferiority in both guns and men. "Lieutenant Turner does us and America proud, Mr. Taylor. See how he rises the <u>Caledonia</u> admirably above her station?"

With that, Perry dismissed the sailing master and returned his attention to the battle at hand. Somewhat luckily for the Americans, the British squadron seemed to be focusing on the already tattered sails instead of the <u>Lawrence</u>'s hull. Perhaps the enemy was more keen to disable the <u>Lawrence</u> and take her a prize than sink her. Hidden in those frayed rags that were once the pristinely white sails Alexander had helped inspect were the marines, hiding in the crow's nest taking mostly potshots at the crew of the <u>Detroit</u>. Their lieutenant, Brooks, leaned over to the commodore and said, "Sir, should we reposition…" but before he could finish a terrible force threw the officer across the deck.

He was too far away for Alexander to hear his shrieks of pain, but the midshipman could easily see the anguish on the lieutenant's face. The physical damage to the normally composed man was devastating. As the officers, including Lieutenant Yarnall and Commodore Perry gathered around their fallen comrade, who had been hit by a piece of round shot in the thigh, shattering his leg. The rest of the battle fell aside as the lieutenant gruffly grabbed his superior officer's coat and pulled him close.

"Comm…arg…sir…this…this…I don't know…know…know…It hurts! Arg! Please, sir…arg!...perform a mercy!"

Alexander knew what Brooks was asking for, but he couldn't believe it. He couldn't imagine a pain so great that the normally stoic and reserved man would beg for his end.

"No, John," Commodore Perry replied, kneeling before the marine and grasping the dying man's hand in his own. "We'll take you to Dr.

Parsons." Brook's head drooped. "Listen to me! The enemy hasn't surrendered to us yet. I can't relieve you of your duty until then." Alexander could see tears welling up in his brother's eyes. "Mr. Taylor! Mr. Perry! Help the lieutenant below deck."

Alexander used all of his strength to help the tall Brooks to his feet, but it was the large Mr. Taylor that gave the marine most of the support as they crossed the increasingly slippery quarterdeck and down the stairs to the makeshift surgery. The cabin was already nearly full with about twenty wounded men in splints and covered in bandages that had already bled through. Yet, despite their injuries, the men looked up at the uninjured men with hope. After wishing Brooks their best and a speedy recovery, these men asked all at once:

"How goes the battle?"

"Are we whipping 'em"

"Is the commodore giving it to them?"

"Should we go back up and help?"

Mr. Taylor assured them that the battle was going well and that the men below deck had no need of proving their courage since it had already been demonstrated before the Almighty.

The <u>Lawrence</u> was built low in the water and the berth deck was already leaking, Alexander sloshed through the water, which was almost up to his ankles. Perry's spaniel, which had been locked up in the captain's cabin startled Alexander and almost made him slip. A round shot had penetrated the hull creating a hole between the cabins that was small enough to see through but not big enough for the dog to pass through. The dog ran back and forth behind that hole, its brown fur brushing up against the arm of the closest seaman laying nearby while the animal barked madly at every blast of cannon. Alexander didn't know the dog well enough to quite figure out if the barking was from fear or anger, but he assumed that it had to be a mixture of both.

He might have laughed at the sight had the injured and agonizing Brooks not been draped over his shoulder. With every shudder that rippled through the ship from every piece of cannon fire both given and received, Brooks grimaced and whimpered.

Dr. Parsons found them and quickly guided the trio to a corner not quite large enough fit the lieutenant's large frame, leaving his feet to find rest upon the legs of an unconscious man with a bandaged head. As Brooks breathed deeply, trying to gain the strength to speak through the pain, Dr. Parsons inspected the lieutenant's injury.

"Usher, be honest with me. Will I make it?"

"I…John, I'm sorry. This is beyond me. You've lost a lot of blood, and I don't think I can stop it."

Brooks nodded his head. "How long, do you think?"

"A few hours…maybe…"

Again Brooks nodded his head. "Anything to drink?"

Dr. Parsons quickly retrieved a clear bottle half full of whiskey and handed it to the dying marine who took a quick gulp and handed the bottle back to the doctor.

"If you can't do anything for me, then leave me be and just let me know what's going on from time to time. Maybe I'll live long enough to hear those bastards surrender."

Sailing Master Taylor gruffly pulled at Alexander's coat and nearly dragged him through the surgery. "Come along, Mr. Perry," he said, "back to your post now." They had to stop and move to the side as a group of wounded men came down at the same time. Two Kentuckians, who seemed somewhat relieved to be a little safer below deck, supported the Indian Charles Pohig who had had his leg amputated cleanly by round shot.

On deck, Alexander saw what first looked like anarchy. Rigging that had been shot from the mast was littering the deck while at least three of the starboard guns were disabled with pieces of their carriages blown apart and scattered in every direction. The deck itself looked as though someone had indiscriminately taken an axe to every plank; chipping, cutting, and tearing at the wood for several hours until the ship resembled a tree struck by lightning more than a naval warship. And yet, discipline remained. The few uninjured men left had stayed at their posts, along with quite a few men with obvious cuts, bruises, and various traumas that they may or may not have actually known they had. At the aft of the vessel knelt the commodore excitedly gesturing to the ten-gun British brig the <u>Hunter</u> which had taken up a position to the <u>Lawrence</u>'s rear and was firing at the American flagship in between volleys with the <u>Caledonia</u> which continued to bravely attract attention from its superior opponents. The commodore squatted as he ordered Dulaney, who had taken charge of the rear starboard carronade along with the rear gun, to fire the rear batteries at the British vessel. Crouching below the constant fire from the enemy ship, both Alexander and the sailing master found their way to their commander.

When the pair were no more than five feet from Commodore Perry, still too far to hear what Perry and Dulaney were shouting at each other, Dulaney quickly stood up, turned as though he were moving from the rear gun to the starboard gun, and promptly fell backwards with tremendous force against a seaman who was crouching behind him. Alexander had already seen Lieutenant Brooks felled by enemy fire, but just a few moments of battle later he now saw his dearest friend and shipmate struck in the same manner. There had been no time to mourn the soon to expire commander of the marines, but, without thinking, Alexander knew that he would need to take some time there, with bullets and cannon shot whizzing inches from his own head, to grieve for his friend.

He closed his eyes as he cradled Dulaney's head in his lap and felt his friend's body shuddering. Alexander thought that it was the final convulsions of life before death took the newly appointed lieutenant, but a quick look down told him the truth. The shuddering of his friend's body was not death's grip wringing life from Dulaney, but Dulaney laughing.

"That hurt like hell!" Dulaney shouted between wheezes for air and fits of laughter.

"What…" began Alexander as he looked down at Dulaney's chest and saw the grapeshot that had spent itself and lodged firmly in his waistcoat.

"Are you hurt, Mr. Forrest?" asked the concerned commodore as he pulled Dulaney to his knees. "That looked quite nasty."

"No, sir. I can stay at my station," replied Dulaney. "I am not hurt, but this," he pulled the pellets from his waistcoat and held them up for everyone to see, "this is *my* shot!"

In the heat of battle, with death and destruction in every direction and without a quiet moment to think, it is strange how odd events can affect the mind of a soldier and seaman. The Lawrence was in desperate battle with little support and, it was becoming increasingly apparent, no path to victory, and yet the commodore, sailing master, second lieutenant, and the commodore's aide stayed for a moment when death could greet them swiftly in order to laugh. It was no chuckle, but a hearty roar of merriment more appropriate for the late hours of a friendly dinner in peacetime than upon a dying ship at war. Alexander couldn't explain it, but for those few seconds the action became secondary and Dulaney's little jest became the most interesting, important, and hilarious thing on Earth.

But, as soon as it began, the joyful display disappeared like a rock tossed into the lake. They thought no more of it and turned all of their attention to the desperate task at hand.

"To your station, Mr. Forrest," said Commodore Perry plainly. "Fight on!"

Dulaney's "aye" was lost in the eruption from his cannon that had been filled with double round shot and aimed directly at one of the Detroit's guns, blasting it beyond repair with a metallic screech.

"Sir!" shouted Taylor to the commodore. "The <u>Niagara</u>! She's still holding back. When will she come into close action to relieve us, sir?" Again, Taylor pointed to the <u>Lawrence</u>'s sister ship more than a mile away which was making little show to help.

"Never mind the <u>Niagara</u>, Mr. Taylor," replied the commodore. "Captain Elliott is a man of experience and knows what he is doing."

"But, sir! You gave him an order!"

"Mr. Taylor!" the commanding officer's tone suddenly sounded sharp and almost angry. "I need your attention here, now, on this ship. I'm losing officers and men. I cannot worry about what I cannot change."

Taylor signaled his acceptance of his commander's rebuke, saluted, and went to see what he could do with the rigging, hoping to be able to get the <u>Lawrence</u> under wind power again.

"Mr. Perry," said the commodore with a firm hand on the midshipman's shoulder. "The third battery is missing a couple of men. I need you to go and get it back to working order."

"Aye, sir," replied Alexander as he prepared to go.

"Also," said Perry with a little tug at Alexander's shoulder, "they're still shooting at her sails. See if you can take out the pilot's station, and then focus on the enemy's guns."

"Aye," and the junior officer was off. As he passed the other manned batteries he passed along Commodore Perry's orders. First was Peleg with a nasty cut from a pistol ball that had grazed his cheek. The midshipman couldn't hear Alexander, but understood enough of Alexander's hand gestures to reposition his gun and fire the next shot into the enemy's deck. Next was Augustus who couldn't raise his right arm or hear from his bleeding right ear, but he could understand well enough from his left and immediately followed orders. The last junior officer before the third gun was Henry who seemed to be mostly deaf by that point, but had gleaned enough from what had been going on down the line to already adjust his tactics.

Alexander's new station had only two seamen to work it, and they were doing their best amid the carnage and chaos of battle. They were Johnson from Kentucky and the Russian, Ivan. Alexander recalled Johnson's fear the day before atop the mast, but none of that trepidation showed on the seaman's face at the moment. His air was placid and workmanlike. He worked the gun as calmly as he would have churned butter at home. Ivan, however, was almost a raving lunatic, shouting so loudly that Alexander could hear snippets of what must have been the vilest Russian profanity as he tried to kill the British with harsh words as much as cannon fire.

Alexander took his new station and began to retarget the gun towards the <u>Detroit</u>'s pilot wheel. The other two men adjusted their tasks as though orders had been cleanly heard and Alexander had been there from the beginning. Alexander worked the cranks on the carronade's carriage and made a quick inspection of the enemy's flagship. It was heavily damaged with rigging in tatters almost as badly as those of the <u>Lawrence</u> and a pulpy mass of wood instead of the clean lines of a freshly hewn hull. The <u>Detroit</u>'s hull stood a few feet taller in the water than that of the <u>Lawrence</u>, so firing upon the pilot's station became a near impossibility without perfect circumstances, so Alexander adjusted again and aimed at the closest gun port. He fired the carronade, making a mighty hole in the enemy's side, but he had missed the gun itself which belched a round shot at the <u>Lawrence</u>'s deck. The ball shattered part of the railing and sent large wooden shards everywhere. Alexander was able to hide behind the gun while his head got doused with water from the bucket Johnson used to cool the hot metal case. He closed his eyes for a second to regain his composure and opened them to find his hat between his knees. Before he popped it back on his head, Alexander noticed a pair of holes. He stuck his fingers through them and realized how closely the musket balls had passed by his head. He rubbed his fingers along his scalp, suddenly finding the spot the balls had passed to be somewhat itchy even though they had not touched him, but there was no time to dwell on it. So Alexander placed the hat atop his head and jumped back to his feet. Johnson was busy reloading the gun while Ivan screamed incomprehensibly in Russian with what sounded like the occasional English "again!" interspersed for good measure while he held desperately onto the rope that would put the carronade back into position. The process was over soon enough, though, and Alexander aimed precisely, anxious to avoid the same mistake. With the rip of the cord, round shot expelled from the gun and the distinct sound of metal crashing into and tearing at metal momentarily screeched above the cacophony of battle.

It became obvious that Alexander's small victory was only part of a larger defeat. The <u>Lawrence</u> had only half of its starboard guns in operation. The larboard side guns had all been galvanized and appropriated to support the side facing the enemy. Both long twelves were useless and only four of the carronades could fire a shot. If the battle had only been between the <u>Lawrence</u> and the <u>Detroit</u>, the Americans might have won the contest, but she couldn't manage much longer with not only the British flagship attacking, but also the support of the <u>Queen Charlotte</u> and the

Hunter, both pummeling the American brig with hardly any other serious adversaries.

Alexander noticed Henry laying on the ground, cradling his arm, and trying to shout orders to what was left of his gun crew.

"Henry!" Alexander shouted trying to grab the other midshipman's attention. "Henry! Your arm!"

Some piece of shrapnel, either flying bits of the deck or a burst enemy ball, had severely broken the young man's arm. A bit of white bone jutted out from Henry's forearm and had torn through his coat.

Alexander grabbed Henry by the shoulders and shouted, "You've broken your arm, Henry!"

Henry looked up at Alexander, and, for a moment, his eyes looked past the junior officer standing above him. "What...?" he began as he focused his eyes and looked down. "My arm! I need a splint! Get Dr. Parsons! I need a splint!"

"He's below," replied Alexander.

"Right," Henry said. He pulled himself up with his good arm and Alexander's support and immediately made for the stairs to the berth deck with a promised shout of return trailing behind him.

Swiftly following the injured midshipman went the commodore himself. Suddenly seized with the fear that his brother had been wounded and was seeking medical aid, Alexander jumped to his feet in pursuit of Oliver. Alexander's older brother was the galvanizing presence on deck. When men fell, all they needed to do was lock eyes with the captain and their souls, lightened of the worries of personal injury, were filled with patriotic fervor and the desire for victory. What would happen to the Lawrence's already precarious position if their guiding light, their cornerstone, their rock went below deck, bleeding and possibly even dying? All of the worst possibilities swept over Alexander as he ran across the deck and dodged musket balls, grape shot, and wood that screamed through the air.

His fears, though, were unfounded. The commodore was uninjured. In fact, Alexander couldn't discern even any holes in his brother's cloak. The young commander leaned his head to be heard below deck and spoke, under the circumstances, almost as though he were asking for extra sugar for his tea. "Doctor," he said, "send me one of your men" Moments later, one of Dr. Parsons assistants came up on deck, listened to Perry's orders which his commander shouted into his ear, and made for one of the three remaining guns, all of which were undermanned. The assistant pushed past Alexander, barely noticing the thirteen year old boy, and joined in the fight.

"Alex!" shouted Oliver as he first noticed his younger brother, suddenly forgetting rank in the midst of battle. "I couldn't…" He broke off as the explosion of another hit rocked the ship and disabled one of the final three guns, along with all of the seamen and officers working it. The commodore turned his attention back to the berth deck and shouted for Dr. Parsons to send another man who quickly found his way on deck and ran to help the final fighting pocket of resistance on the ship. As Perry turned back to Alexander, his eyes full of brotherly affection, an even closer explosion rocked the ship, and a half-second later, Alexander felt a thud against the back of his head.

The midshipman opened his eyes groggily, as though someone was shaking him awake before the break of dawn, but it wasn't the light of morning that he saw. His eyes slowly focused and he realized that he was looking at the clear blue sky through the last fragments of the Lawrence's rigging and sails. Sound came back immediately, but it was hard to tell if the commodore, who was leaning over Alexander, shouting, was making the explosion sounds or the words. "Are you alive?" After a moment, the disorientation passed and Alexander was able to respond.

"I'll be fine. I'm fine. What happened?" he asked as he cradled the back of his head and looked around him. Wreckage was everywhere, and the ship looked even worse than he remembered from moments before. More broken wood, more twisted metal, more holes, and more bodies. And above it all, as his eyes finally focused completely, Alexander saw snow falling from the sky.

"The hammocks," said the commodore. "The enemy hit the hammocks, and they exploded. You must have been whacked on the head by some soft shard." His smile was broad and genuine.

Alexander reached out and snatched some of the snow from the air. It was soft and warm instead of cold and wet.

"It's the down, the feathers from the bedding," said Oliver with a laugh.

"Sir," came the voice of Lieutenant Yarnall. Alexander looked up at the second-in-command and almost burst into laughter. The only thing that stopped him was the dull pounding on the back of his head. However the commodore was uninhibited by injury and mirthfully greeted his first officer. Yarnall held himself as professionally as he always did, but he was covered in the down feathers. His coat was wet with spray and his head was soaked with sweat and blood from a wound on his forehead the feathers stuck to all of it.

"Lieutenant Owl," said Perry with a jocular smile, "what can I do for you? Perhaps I could find you some grubs and chubs to feast on?"

"Sir, I don't think…" began Yarnall, embarrassed.

"Of course. I beg your pardon, John."

"Aye, sir," replied Yarnall moving on from the jest. "I require more men to man the guns. Most of my officers are dead or below deck awaiting Dr. Parsons."

"I apologize, John, but you must endeavor to make out yourself: I have no more to furnish you." The commodore peeked over the barrels that were giving the little group their cover against the enemy's fire. "We fought well, men." He looked back over to the southeast and the Lawrence's sister ship still standing tall and untouched.

"We're not giving up, are we, sir?" asked Yarnall. Despite the blood and lives lost, there was not a man on that ship that wanted to raise the white flag.

Perry looked at his first officer with a knowing smile. "Lieutenant Yarnall, do you think that I could ever let that flag fall in battle under my command?" he asked pointing to the 15 starred and 15 striped banner of the United States that flew from the mainmast.

"Of course not, sir," replied Yarnall, the color quickly returning to his face.

Dulaney sprinted into the group, colliding with Alexander, throwing the midshipman to the deck. "Sorry…sorry…sir…That brig will not help us!" he said pointing to the Niagara. "See how he keeps off, he will not come to close action."

"I'll fetch him up," replied the commodore, his smile still planted firmly across his face.

CHAPTER VI: Tactical Retreat

2 P.M.

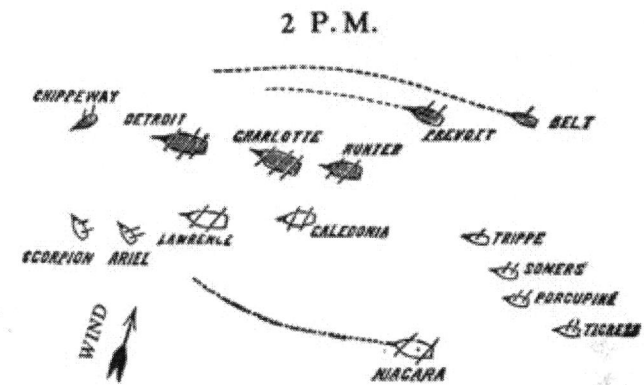

"2 P.M." from *The Naval War of 1812* by Theodore Roosevelt

Alexander had read several books on historical naval battles and had heard tales of marital bravery on the high seas for his whole life, but he had never heard of a captain transferring his command from one crippled vessel to a fresh one in the middle of an engagement. It must have been pure luck that the dinghy hanging on the back of the <u>Lawrence</u> was, for all intents and purposes, unharmed and seaworthy. The battle continued on the <u>Lawrence</u> as marines laid fire to anything that moved on the deck of the British ships and the few remaining cannons on the <u>Detroit</u> and <u>Queen Charlotte</u> fired at whatever targets they could find. The environment made it both dangerous and difficult to get the small rowboat into the water while seamen ran out to prepare it for the lake. The process only took a few minutes: minutes that felt like hours to Alexander especially when Johnson the Kentuckian, and the only member of Alexander's gun crew still uninjured at his post, ran out to secure the tackle. With a hollow but heavy splash the dinghy fell into the water, still unharmed as though the enemy couldn't see, reach, or bring itself to care about the small vessel.

His task completed, Alexander ran down to the captain's cabin to find the commodore who had gone to take care of some ship's business before setting off. The cabin was a wreck like the rest of the ship. It was difficult to tell whether the wreckage had been legs of chairs, bits of the hull, or pieces of shrapnel. Sometimes, it seemed as though chunks were several at once, the result of iron crashing into the <u>Lawrence</u> near the shot's melting point from an overheated barrel, fusing the heavy round ball with several pieces of wood from different sources at once.

Commodore Perry stood by the small kitchen with a fire burning in the oven as he shoved envelopes and letters into the flames. Lieutenant Yarnall, who had found a bandage for his forehead and plucked most of the feathers off, hauled a small metal box to the window, its glass shattered across the floor, and tossed the chest out into the lake below. It contained the official papers of the ship, sent to the bottom of the lake to avoid their capture, but preserved in the hope that they could be retrieved later.

"Are you ready, sir?" asked Yarnall as he rubbed his hands together to get rid of the dirt from the box.

The commodore had a bunch of papers in one hand and a single letter in his right. Without hesitation he threw the bundle into the fire, but he held onto the single piece of paper for a moment longer. Peering at the writing, Alexander saw the familiar script of his sister-in-law. Perry stalled for a moment more, squeezed the paper between his finger like he was trying to push the words from his wife into his skin, and tossed the final message into the oven.

"The boat's ready, sir," said Alexander, saddened by the sight he had just witnessed yet did not quite understand.

A second later, the commodore turned to his first officer and aide with a smile once again across his face. "Very good, gentlemen." They began to walk out of the captain's cabin and the commodore spoke as they made their exit. "It's up to you, John, to fight as much longer as you feel capable. Just remember, we've fought well, and there is no dishonor in striking the colors after the fight we've put up. I might just ask for enough time and cover to make it to the <u>Niagara</u>."

"We'll do our best, sir," replied Yarnall.

"Very good. It's all I can ask for."

"What, sir," began Yarnall with a hand on the commodore's shoulder, boldly stopping him. "What will you say to Captain Elliott?" he asked referring to the captain of the <u>Niagara</u>.

Perry took a quick moment to look into his first officer's eyes. It was fleeting, but Alexander sensed that Yarnall's bravery died quickly. He almost imperceptibly slouched and cast his eyes down in shame.

"The first thing I shall say to him, Mr. Yarnall, is 'Good afternoon.'"

With that, Perry bounded up the stairs to the main deck with Alexander and Yarnall right behind. The dinghy was already populated by seven men. They were a ragtag bunch, almost none of whom had gone uninjured in the course of battle. Almost half were Kentuckians that Alexander did not know, but he recognized James Campbell, the Irishman from Baltimore, Hannibal Collins, Thomas Breese, and Ivan the Russian who held the blue flag with the last words of Captain Lawrence emblazoned upon it, neatly folded in his lap.

Dulaney found Alexander before he could climb into the dingy ahead of Commodore Perry. They had seen each other only a few minutes before, but it felt like days since they last teased and felt at ease with each other.

"Good luck, Alex," said Dulaney, shaking the young midshipman's hand firmly.

"You too, Lieutenant," replied Alexander.

With that, Alexander bounded down the rope ladder into the boat and sat in the empty seat by Hannibal Collins.

"Think you're strong enough to row?" asked the seaman.

"I think we're going to need every arm, no matter how small."

Hannibal laughed lightly and patted Alexander on the shoulder. "Good one, little sir. That we will."

Perry stood on the top rung of the ladder, giving final instructions to Yarnall. They saluted each other and separated. Yarnall took command of the Lawrence and Perry descended into the dingy. He remained standing as he helped push off from the shattered bones of what had once been his command.

The men in the boat began to row, including Alexander, away from the Lawrence and towards the Niagara which seemed to have finally found the wind and was sailing in the direction of the battle, exchanging largely ineffective shots with its two long guns as the British squadron continued to focus the bulk of its diminished efforts mostly on the Lawrence and, to a lesser extent, the smaller Caledonia which was still trying to attract attention from the British. The further the dingy got from the center of battle, the more clearly it became obvious how much damage the Lawrence had sustained. Its foremast had been shot apart and only rags and tatters of the rigging and sails hung, limply flapping in the wind, from the tall wooden beams. The hull had dozens of holes on its ports side from round shot that had passed straight through the ship. The clean lines that had been there only that morning had become twisted, bent, and broken by the constant barrage of the last two hours. She was scarred and brutalized, the same as the ship's crew. Out of the hundred men who had taken an active part in the battle, the early count had it at nineteen dead and at least fifty wounded. Henry Laub had been struck by a cannonball almost as soon as he had gone below deck. Charles Pohig, the carpenter's mate, had died helping another seaman up after an explosion had thrown him to the deck. Augustus might need to have his arm amputated because of the musket ball that had lodged itself there like a leaden tick. Alexander almost felt guilty for getting off of the ship with only a bruised head.

Commodore Perry remained standing as the boat pulled further from the Lawrence. His eyes were fixed upon the vessel, inspecting every hurt, probably cataloging them in his mind for future reference when they would take her back into port for repairs. After a few minutes, they cleared the Lawrence's hull and came into sight of the Queen Charlotte's cannons. The battle had by then largely quieted down. Gone was the steady and almost methodical beat of precisely timed firing from both the American and British ships. Most of the guns had been destroyed or merely disabled leading the strong drum of cannon and carronade to no longer being dominated by the sounds of battle but by the distant crack of small arms popping shots from the across the water. However, when the Queen Charlotte let lose a broadside at the dinghy bobbing its way through the water, that new façade of manageable calm came crashing down.

The men pulling the small vessel along had been hoping that the British might ignore them or even confuse them with the flotsam floating out from the center of battle. There were other large pieces of wood and even corpses drifting about, but the crew of the boat had known that the enemy would discover them soon enough which the broadside had quickly confirmed. None of the round shot hit or even came particularly close, but a couple of the cannons must have been filled with grapeshot. None of the tiny lead bits hit any of the men because the enemy had aimed too low, but some of the sailors nearly jumped from their seats when the hard sound of metal pellets striking the wooden hull of the boat sent a shockwave through the paneling. Very soon thereafter the crack of small arms gained a more sinister character as the crew of the Queen Charlotte, joined in by that of the Hunter, began to fire their rifles at the dingy.

Thomas Breese, who seemed more at ease with the situation than anyone else on that boat aside from the commodore, leaned forward and tapped Alexander on the back. While trying to maintain his rowing motion, the midshipman turned to the chaplain.

"How old are you, Mr. Perry? If I had to venture a guess, I'd say no more than eleven."

The out of place question might have been confusing, but Alexander found himself automatically replying deferentially. "I'm thirteen, sir."

"Still, that's quite young, especially for one who remained so calm throughout that mayhem."

"Really?" asked Alexander turning to Hannibal to see his thoughts.

The former slave shrugged as if to say, "He didn't need to tell me."

"*Bien sure*," replied Breese without even attempting a French accent. "I got to huddle at the aft of the ship with a couple of large guns to keep me company, but you were everywhere and you didn't even seem to notice the danger you were in most of the time."

Alexander thought back. He could have sworn that he had been terrified throughout the entire affair, but he couldn't remember actually doing anything but following orders.

"If you ask me," continued Breese, "you acted like a man twice your age and with a dozen battles hard fought behind you."

"I don't think I need to say it, little sir," added Hannibal, "but he's right."

Alexander could find no words, so he beamed with pride at the kind words from his elders. Quickly, though, the reality of their situation came back to the junior officer as a single musket ball splashed into the lake only a few feet away and sprayed them with a cool mist of water, dousing his thoughts and bringing him back to the task at hand.

Through all of this, Commodore Perry remained standing, studying the damage to the Lawrence as well as what damage the Americans had inflicted on the British squadron. Through the smoke and din of direct battle it had been difficult to find either the time or the opportunity to look beyond the hull of the Lawrence, but in the open water it became much easier to see that in front of them had been the American Ariel and the Scorpion engaging with the British vessels the Chippewa and the Little Belt to largely little effect. Behind the American flagship the Somers, Porcupine, Tigress, and the Trippe were still trying to catch up and the Niagara was finally making its way into close action. At the center of the engagement lay a sight of pure destruction. The Lawrence had, for two hours, taken the vast majority of fire from the three largest British vessels, the Detroit, Hunter, and Queen Charlotte with the Lady Prevost fighting both the Lawrence and the Ariel and the Scorpion in front. The wreckage, mostly of the Lawrence, was spreading outward like oil on the water. It was as though a mighty titan had plucked the brig out of the lake, crushed it nimbly with one hand, shaken it in the air, and dropped it unceremoniously back into the water. And yet, the battle had not yet ended. The Lawrence still flew the American flag on its mast, and in between finding cover and firing pot shots at the British, the crew looked earnestly out across the water at the little boat filled with their fellow seaman, huddled as far down into the boat as possible while still being able to row, and a single standing figure towering above them: Oliver Hazard Perry.

"Commodore!" pleaded Alexander. "Please sit down!"

"Very good," replied Perry absentmindedly, his eyes squinting and his fingers trying to count the guns on the <u>Queen Charlotte</u>.

Another broadside from the <u>Queen Charlotte</u> tore through the air, this one much better aimed. The heavy whir of round shot zipped by the crew's heads, passing close enough to hit a couple of extended oars, shattering the wooden paddles and tearing them from the hands of the seamen who held them. Some of the shot missed low, but close enough to spray the whole boat with fresh water and rock the vessel side to side.

Perry, lost in his battlefield study and unable to discern the danger to himself, pointed towards the British line. "Yes, I think I see it..." he began as though he were continuing a conversation he had been having with himself in his head, but before he could finish, another series of rifle fire arose from the <u>Queen Charlotte</u>, prompting Alexander to take quick action. He grabbed his brother's coat and pulled him down into the boat with all of his strength. The violent movement didn't even faze the commodore. He continued to study the British line for a moment more before he turned to his brother, his eyes looking through him, and said, "I need to get on board the <u>Niagara</u>."

The boat was soon within half-pistol shot of the <u>Niagara</u>, much too far from any of the British vessels for rifle fire to actually reach them, and with every passing moment it became more obvious that the British had lost interest in wasting their dwindling supply of ammunition on a tiny dinghy. The seamen began to relax and talk again. Very quickly the small conversations turned to Captain Elliott.

"Where has he been?"

"It's dereliction it is."

"...cowardly and craven..."

"...court marshal..."

"I hope they hang 'em. Left us to die."

Commodore Perry awoke from his studious trance long enough to hear the talk. "Concentrate on rowing the boat," he said plainly but forcefully, his eyes hard with anger at the insubordination he had just heard. Alexander didn't know exactly what Perry was thinking of Elliott keeping the <u>Niagara</u> out of the fight against orders, but he had an idea of how his brother thought in general. Commodore Perry was methodical and wanted as much information as he could gain before making the kinds of decisions that could ruin the lives of men, especially men he respected like Captain Elliott, but above all, Perry respected the chain of command. If Captain Elliott had disobeyed orders, it was the job of his commanding officer to address that, not the men serving under him.

"Signal the Niagara that I'm coming aboard, Mr. Perry," said the commodore.

"Aye, sir," replied Alexander. With the firing upon the dingy subsided, Alexander felt much more at ease standing and making a show than he would have a mere few minutes before. He told the midshipman on deck through hand signals the commodore's intentions. The young officer (who was still probably older than Alexander) replied with the signal that they were letting down the ladder. At the same time, a collective groan arose from the sailors in the dinghy.

"What is it?" asked Alexander quickly turning to Hannibal.

"The Lawrence, she's struck," replied the sailor.

Alexander turned to the flagship to see the American stars and stripes descending the mast. It was a sight Alexander had known was inevitable. The ship had no guns left. It was little more than a floating hulk of wood and torn sail, so much less than when it had first sailed from Pennsylvania just weeks before.

"We'll still win the day," said Commodore Perry in reply. "Can you hear it?" he asked. "They're cheering. The enemy thinks that they have won. They seem to have forgotten our sister ship. but we haven't have we?"

The sailors smiled as they looked into their commodore's eyes. Alexander felt the same thing they did: hope.

They soon came up against the Niagara's port side. One of the Kentuckians grabbed hold of the rope ladder dangling from the brig's hull and brought the dinghy against it, the wooden frame of the rowboat gently knocking against the larger ship. Looking out over the lake as Perry took the ladder, Alexander was struck by how calm the sight seemed. The smoke of battle rolled lazily off the distant wreckage of the Lawrence with the British vessels floating nearby. The few remaining guns that pounded shot at each other between the smaller ships felt muffled and distant. It was almost like looking at a painting.

A moment later, Perry was up the ladder and Alexander followed. The Niagara and the Lawrence had been built at the same time by the same hands from the same plans. They were identical twins, but one was sitting half a mile away, bleeding out, while the other had stood by and only watched the beating her sister had received. Alexander had been too hurried, scared, and tired to sort his thoughts into anything resembling neat for some time, but when he saw Captain Elliot, his hat at his side in deference to his commanding officer, his wispy patch of hair flapping heedlessly in the breeze, and his uniform pristinely clean more than two hours into a desperate battle, Alexander clearly felt rage pierce through everything else. Suddenly, Alexander found himself understanding what the sailors had been saying of Elliott in the dinghy.

"How goes the day, Commodore?" asked Elliott, the words sending a pulsing spike of heat up Alexander's spine.

"Badly," replied Perry. "I have lost most of my men to the enemy's guns. I left Lieutenant Yarnall in charge of the <u>Lawrence</u>, but she was a wreck when I left, and Yarnall has struck her colors." Perry fell silent and an uncomfortable quiet fell between the two men. Alexander looked up at his commander and saw, not rage, but something far more familiar. It was the same look of disappointment their mother would use on them when her children had misbehaved. On Oliver's face, at that moment, it seemed that their mother was there, ready to scold Elliott with a soft but firmly felt reprimand. Perry turned to the east, pointed at the trailing schooners and sloops, and asked, "Mr. Elliott, what are the gunboats doing so far astern?"

Captain Elliott began to open his mouth, ready to offer an excuse, but he thought better of it and closed his mouth. A moment more of eerie stillness passed before Elliott replied, "Perhaps, I'll go and bring them up."

"Very good," replied Perry simply.

Elliott quickly gathered one of the <u>Niagara</u>'s midshipmen and several able-bodied seamen and climbed into the boat Perry had rowed through the danger of battle.

As the boat became ready to push off, Perry leaned over taffrail and said, "It may not look it, Mr. Elliott, but we are close to victory. Distract the enemy as much as possible and prevent them from escaping. This battle should be over soon."

"Aye, sir," said Elliott perfunctorily, and, with that, the captain of the <u>Niagara</u> had left his ship to find another command on board the <u>Somers</u>.

With Elliott gone, the tension and anger slowly began to fade from Alexander's mind. In time, Perry's final words to the <u>Niagara</u>'s captain actually sank in. Victory was at hand? The <u>Lawrence</u> was disabled and useless, the British still had all of their ships in the fight including the <u>Detroit</u> which had been imposing before but seemed almost invincible after taking out the <u>Lawrence</u>.

"Mr. Edwards," Perry said to the <u>Niagara</u>'s first lieutenant as the commodore approached the pilot's station with Alexander in tow, "are you ready to engage the enemy?"

The young man smiled broadly at his new commander, his face red from the sun, spray, and wind while his blond hair gently swayed in the breeze. "Aye, sir!" he replied enthusiastically.

"Very good. Straight at 'em, Mr. Edwards. Straight at 'em."

CHAPTER VII: Headfirst

2:50 P.M.

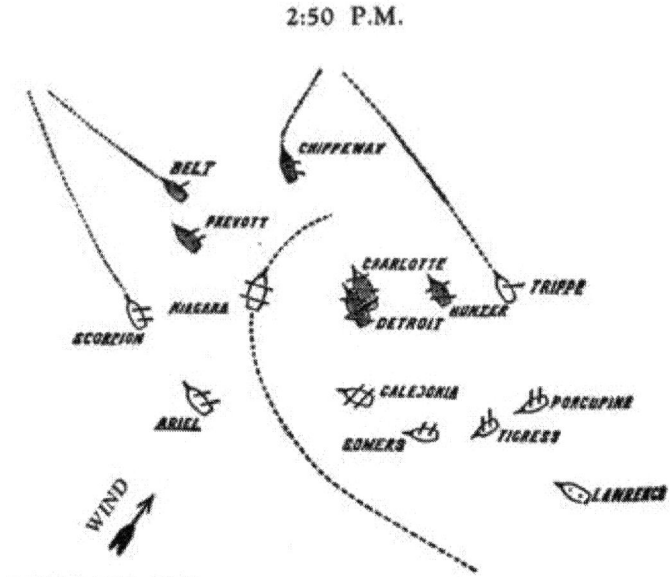

"2:50 P.M." from *The Naval War of 1812* by Theodore Roosevelt

First was to hoist the blue battle flag up the <u>Niagara</u>'s mast. Under orders, Alexander retrieved the flag from Hannibal and took it to the ship's sailing master, Nelson Webster, a short stocky man, who quickly sent the flag to join the stars and stripes flapping valiantly in the wind which had shifted to the northwest. The crew cheered the standard, recognizing Captain Lawrence's words and obviously anxious to end their roles as spectators, to fight alongside their brethren at last.

Alexander returned to the pilot's station to find that Perry was already amidst a mad torrent of orders to get the <u>Niagara</u> into action.

"Back the main topsail!" which would stop the brig from drifting away from the battle. "Braid up the main topsail!" he continued. "Put the helm up and bear down before the wind. Mr. O'Neil," he ordered the pilot. "Set the top-gallant sails and heave to for close action!"

The crew of the <u>Niagara</u> moved with the fresh clip one would expect from an untouched warship. They jumped at every order with excitement and earnestness. They knew where they were going, and they could feel victory in Commodore Perry's words.

Alexander was standing by the starboard gunwale looking out at the Lawrence when one of the Niagara's midshipmen, Samuel Adams, a lad of fourteen from New York, approached Alexander and asked, "What was it like?"

Alexander looked at the young man with ginger hair and saw the youth in his eyes. Thinking about it for a quick second, Alexander realized that he must have had the same look just a few hours before. Alexander had lived through more than two hours of fire, smoke, blood, and death, and at that moment, he mostly just felt numb. He had seen suffering and destruction that he would never be able to forget. He had seen one of the final moments of Henry Laub's life, the life of someone who had become a good friend over the last few months. He knew that later would come guilt at having lived without any sort of injury through all of that, but for the moment, all he could feel was the spray of lake water against his cheek. All he could smell was the mix of gunpowder residue and fresh air. All he could see was the British fleet against calm water and a blue autumn day.

After what couldn't have been more than a moment, Alexander replied, "Be glad you weren't in it."

"What do you mean?" asked Samuel innocently.

"I mean that we lost almost two thirds of the crew and officers."

"That many?"

"I don't think I've ever read of a naval battle with casualties that high."

"Is Augustus…did he…?" asked Samuel about his fellow New Yorker. The two hadn't known each other before their posting to Erie while the sister brigs were under construction, but they had quickly taken to each other because of their shared home state.

"I think he had some scrapes the last time I saw him, but nothing serious."

"Good, good," replied Samuel, his mind quickly turning to other things. "When it starts," he continued, "will it be like our practice runs? Will it be that loud?"

"More than that, "Alexander replied, recalling the foggy hell of battle. "Imagine the racket of a couple dozen cannons throwing metal at each other, and, instead of the shot falling harmlessly a mile out to sea, they tear through wood and iron. And if you thought the smoke was bad before, you can't even see what you're firing at after a couple of minutes even when the other ship is less than a hundred yards away." He worried that they were going to sail right back into it. Into the fire, smoke, blood, and death. He looked to his brother and hoped that he had been right when he had told Elliott that victory was at hand.

Samuel lost the color in his face. He had obviously listened too closely to newspaper men's accounts of battle instead of those who had seen it themselves. Alexander had grown up knowing that there was both glory and tragedy, each messy and broken, during war, but Samuel had come to a real fight thinking that wars were clean. He should have known better, especially after spending months with battle tested sailors at Erie, but no matter what, the young man was going to learn the reality soon enough.

Alexander turned his attention to the <u>Detroit</u> which was coming into view out from behind the wreckage of the <u>Lawrence</u>, and saw more activity on the deck of the British flagship than he had expected. It felt more than just unusual.

"Do you have a glass?" he asked Samuel.

Samuel mumbled an affirmative and handed over his personal eyepiece. It was made of silver and polished very finely so it glinted in the sun. It must have been a present from some rich relative. Alexander took the expensive instrument and used it to inspect the <u>Detroit</u>'s crew. Panic had struck the British sailors. They were running around the deck disorderly and without a single purpose. There seemed to be a general desire to secure the mainsail and get the ship moving again, but there remained no steering hand to guide the action. Alexander scanned the deck and realized that he couldn't find any officers except a single midshipman who was trying desperately to create order from the chaos, but the junior officer, who seemed even younger than Alexander, couldn't get the thirty and forty year old hands to listen to him.

Alexander quickly turned and marched to the commodore.

"Hey! That's *my* glass!" said Samuel in a hushed whisper

Alexander thought nothing of it and mindlessly tossed the telescope back to the midshipman. Both the toss and Samuel's attempt at catching it were poorly aimed leading to the expensive piece clattering against the deck, probably scuffing up the soft metal. Alexander would need to apologize later, but there was no time for it now. The knot in his stomach told him to move quickly.

"Sir," said Alexander as he approached Commodore Perry with a quick salute, "the <u>Detroit</u>, sir. I don't think she has any more deck officers."

The commodore had been looking out over the field with his own glass when the midshipman made his report. Without looking down, Perry replied, "Is that so?" as he brought his attention to the <u>Detroit</u>. After a quick moment, Perry finished scanning the deck and said, "That certainly illuminates things. Mr. Edwards," he continued addressing the first officer, "Take us through their line."

Breaking the line. They had talked about it the day before, but it had felt like little more than idle chatter. The entire time they had been on the <u>Niagara</u>, Alexander hadn't even thought of the maneuver, much less noticed the opportunity for it. In almost near disbelief Alexander looked out over the lake, searching for that opening, but he couldn't see it. Even then, after two hours of intense action, there didn't seem to be a large enough gap in the British line for the American brig to pass through, despite the jumble of the original order of battle. After anxiously looking for some moments, Alexander finally found it. The <u>Lady Prevost</u> and <u>Little Belt</u>, over the course of the last two hours, had moved from their position aft of the <u>Detroit</u> and <u>Queen Charlotte</u> to their fore. The two and the <u>Chippewa</u> still had intact sails and were moving with the wind, making no effort to slow down or turn. However, directly behind, in the <u>Detroit</u>, chaos still reigned. Her sails were largely shot away so she couldn't capture the wind, and the distance between the British flagship and the <u>Lady Prevost</u> was growing. And yet, there was still the <u>Queen Charlotte</u> which was largely in as good shape as when the battle had begun. All she needed to do was pass from behind the <u>Detroit</u> on the flagship's starboard quarter and she could close the gap in just a few minutes. If the Commodore hadn't noticed the potential action minutes before and only when Alexander had, there wouldn't have been even the hope of enough time to successfully cut the enemy's line. Even then, they only had a few minutes before the <u>Queen Charlotte</u> could bring up her broadside and ruin the opportunity.

"I think the <u>Detroit</u> has noticed us, sir," said Lieutenant Edwards, pointing towards the vessel. "She seems to be trying to present."

"Look at that pandemonium," replied Perry almost sadly. "It seems safe to assume that Commodore Barclay is no longer giving orders. Very good…although…I do hope nothing serious has happened to him. I've very much looked forward to meeting him."

"Sir?" asked Edwards.

"Barclay was at Trafalgar," Perry explained as though he were at the dinner table, not the pilot's station moving into battle. "Just imagine what he could teach us of that fight that is in no book. Beside, I've always heard that he is a very well-bred and knowledgeable man. Wouldn't you want to meet a man such as that?"

"I suppose so, sir," replied the lieutenant, his face slightly screwed up in confusion.

The <u>Detroit</u> let out a few scattered shots, most of which missed with only a couple that bounced harmlessly off the <u>Niagara</u>'s hull. Alexander shuddered as the echo of the ball's impact flew through him. It was starting again.

"What do you think, Mr. Perry?" asked the commodore.

"Sir?" replied Alexander trying to keep his voice free of fear.

"The enemy's shots seem to be proving ineffective. Why do you think that is?"

Alexander blinked and opened his eyes as though he were waking up from a dream. He thought hard and fast. Based on the <u>Detroit</u>'s firing at the beginning of battle, it was obvious that she was stocked with mostly long guns that could easily reach the Americans at their current distant. "They're not using enough powder?" answered Alexander, completely unsure of his answer.

"A reasonable supposition. What do you think of Mr. Perry's assessment, Mr. Edwards?"

The lieutenant continued to study the enemy when he replied, "That seems most likely. Either they're rationing the powder to the point of ineffectiveness or they're panicking and just not using enough. What…sir, can you see this?"

"What is it, Mr. Edwards?"

"I don't think the <u>Queen Charlotte</u> gave enough room for their passing. I think she's going to hit the <u>Detroit</u>."

Alexander looked out across the water and tried to see what Edwards had described. He was either too short or too unaccustomed to finding order amongst wrecked ships to see what the lieutenant had seen, but the creaking sound of two large wooden vessels crashing against one another was all the confirmation he needed. The two largest British ships had collided, and after a minute of squinting through the mass of torn sails, Alexander could see that the two ships' riggings were cut up, tangled, and hopelessly enmeshed in each other.

"It's going to take some time to sort that out, sir," said Edwards with a smirk.

"Very true. Take us in, Mr. Edwards. Are both batteries ready to fire?"

"Have been for more than two hours, sir."

"Well, I'm glad that we're finding opportunity for the crew of the <u>Niagara</u> to show the British their mettle."

Edwards' smile broadened at the words of this commodore. "Aye, sir."

A tense moment passed. Still the <u>Niagara</u> hadn't fired a shot since Perry had taken command, but she was still under sporadic fire from the rear guns on the <u>Lady Prevost</u> and the few remaining larboard guns on the <u>Detroit</u>. However, the <u>Lady Prevost</u> couldn't hit the American brig, and the <u>Detroit</u> couldn't move to change her position, so the <u>Niagara</u> passed steadily out of her line of sight. The crew on the American brig were silent, but their thirst to lay a decisive blow in the battle after having sat most of it out was nearly as evident as the cries of battle coming from the British vessels.

In that moment, Alexander looked out over the deck of the <u>Niagara</u>. It was all the same but different. There was where his gun crew had fought, but its guns were different with different names and manned by strange sailors. He looked up into the sails, the same sails he had inspected just the day before, but they weren't the same. Or were they? Had the fight on the <u>Lawrence</u> he remembered been just a dream? His heart sank as he looked out at the broken hull of the <u>Lawrence</u> and the realization that it was going to erupt again came to him fully.

Soon, both the <u>Lady Prevost</u> and the <u>Little Belt</u> were squarely in the <u>Niagara</u>'s larboard sights while the desperate mess that was the <u>Detroit</u> and the <u>Queen Charlotte</u> was in the starboard sights.

"Fire, Mr. Edwards," said Perry calmly and comfortably.

The familiar explosion of gunpowder expelling iron balls from iron tubes ending with the cracking destruction of British hulls filled the air. They were at close quarters, about fifty yards away from the enemy's flagship, their fire tearing new holes in the ships fore, the devastation of which Alexander had never experienced so quickly or so forcefully. To the larboard, the British schooner and sloop were further away, but the wrecking of their sterns was no less impressive.

As the crew of the <u>Niagara</u> reloaded the carronades, the crack of rifles filled the air from both the American brig and the British squadron. Marines in the crow's nest of every vessel fired at the crew and officers on deck of their opposing ships. The shots were quick and poorly aimed as the riflemen quickly ducked back under cover avoid the shots from the other side, but some did find their marks. One British ball tore into Lieutenant Edwards's arm, slashing through his jacket and ripping the man's flesh.

Edwards let out a cry of pain as he grasped his arm. He tottered on his feet without falling and bent forwards, breathing heavily and starring at the sand covered deck at his feet.

"Lieutenant!" Alexander shouted as he jumped to his senior's aid.

"Is it bad?"

Edwards gritted his teeth and nodded. He removed his hand, red with blood seeping slowly between his fingers, and looked at the wound beneath. The ball had deeply grazed him, sending a chunk of flesh from his arm. If the ball had hit an inch to the left, it would have probably shattered the bone which would have most likely led to an amputation. Edwards smiled through his grimace and at his good luck.

"I'll be fine, Mr. Perry," replied Edwards. "It was the shock more than anything."

Commodore Perry looked at his injured lieutenant, torn between lending a helping hand or continuing to lead the ship at such a critical moment. Edwards saw the look in his commodore's eyes and waved him away.

"Do you need to go to the doctor?" asked Alexander as he grew anxious at the state of battle.

"No," replied Edwards, shaking his head. "Would *you* go below deck *now*?" His eyes were wide and filled with anticipation.

"Never, sir," said Alexander, smiling at the lieutenant's energy and verve.

"I thought not. Now, help me and find me something to tie this really quickly."

Alexander did as he was bid, helping Edwards by finding and tearing a rag from storage. Edwards took the cloth and tied it around his wounded arm using his teeth as leverage. He and Alexander were back at the commodore's side just as he ordered the second volley.

The Niagara had passed the fore of the Detroit and the Queen Charlotte, sending the broadside directly into the Queen Charlotte's starboard. The American and British ships were so close that the round shot passed straight through the bulwarks of both enmeshed enemy ships, the missiles endangering the smaller American vessels behind that were finally up and giving fight to the British rear.

That final volley was apparently enough for the enemy. Amidst the shouting of the Niagara's crew, the screeches of rope against wooden pulleys as the gun crews fought against time to reload the carronades, and the crack of American rifles, a single British officer appeared on the Queen Charlotte's taffrail with a white cloth in hand.

"They've struck!"

CHAPTER VIII: Evening

Perry's Victory on Lake Erie by Thomas Birch

The chaos of battle melted away, replaced by the bedlam of victory. All firing on the <u>Niagara</u> ended. The quieting of the American guns revealed that all of the firing that continued was at least half a mile away between the American latecomers and the rear of the enemy's line. Cheers erupted from the American sailors as they threw their caps into the air and embraced each other, but a firm look from Perry kept the officers from joining in on the celebration. Alexander knew why: It would be inappropriate for officers to let the crew see them in such a state. Besides, the <u>Queen Charlotte</u> might have surrendered, but there were half a dozen more enemy vessels that needed addressing.

Part of their worries, though, quickly took care of themselves. Within moments of the <u>Queen Charlotte</u> striking her colors, the <u>Detroit</u> had also lowered her Union Jack. Seconds later the <u>Hunter</u> and the <u>Lady Prevost</u> also signaled their surrender.

"Congratulations, Commodore," said Lieutenant Edwards, shaking Perry's hand with a broad smile.

"Thank you," replied Perry, his attention drawn to the two remaining British vessels the <u>Little Belt</u> and the <u>Chippewa</u> which had turned from the battle and seemed to be attempting an escape. "I don't think that our work is quite finished yet, though."

Edwards followed Perry's gaze and noticed the two ships heading north. "Do you think Captain Elliot will pursue?" the lieutenant asked without trying to hide his disdainful tone.

Either Perry ignore the small insubordination from his lieutenant or his mind was too busy to notice because he said nothing of it. He watched the enemy quietly for a moment. "Send the signal for pursuit, if you please."

"Aye, sir."

Perry turned to the lieutenant and remembered the officer's injury. "And go see the surgeon."

This was where the histories usually ended, but Alexander couldn't just close the cover and go to bed.

"What do we do now, sir?" Alexander asked, curious as to what came next.

"First, we secure the area, and then we will receive the enemy's commanders for their formal surrenders."

It took some minutes to get the crew back under control, but soon the cheering ended and the soaring mood returned to earth. It was hard work to propel a five-hundred-ton vessel across the water, and just the prospect of managing the task seemed overwhelming after the ordeal Alexander had just lived through. However, the Niagara already had a full compliment and Alexander was a bit redundant so he stayed close to the commodore, shadowing his movements and leaning against any nearby solid surface, exhaustion soon filtering through the dissipating excitement. It wasn't the kind of weariness he found at the end of a normal day that easily led to sleep. Instead, it just felt like his body was failing to perform basic functions without serious effort. Things like walking and even listening to what other people said had become chores.

"Ahoy!" came a voice from the water below. Alexander walked over and looked over the taffrail to find Captain Elliott in the same small boat Perry had taken from the Lawrence. "Permission to come aboard," cried the Niagara's captain.

Commodore Perry came and stood beside Alexander to welcome the returning captain. Perry had a benign smile on his face, but his eyes sparkled with joy. Apparently any thought of Elliott's failure to bring the Niagara into close action had disappeared as the reality of victory had swept over him. His hands shivered slightly in nervous excitement as he grasped the taffrail and said, "Permission granted."

On board the Niagara, Captain Elliot was far more subdued than the commodore. Elliott's face was sullen almost as though weights were pulling down on his features creating a misshapen grimace. As Alexander took in the mixture of emotions that was the <u>Niagara</u>'s original captain, the fury that had previously filled the midshipman began to swell back, fighting through the nearly complete joy that had overcome him at the sight of the enemy striking their colors and the ensuing fatigue that had overwhelmed him.

The commodore obviously did not share Alexander's mix of feelings and nearly embraced the returning captain. However, Perry regained his composure and merely returned Elliott's salute.

"Congratulations, sir, on such a tremendous victory," said Elliott, his voice flat and nearly characterless.

"Thank you, Captain," replied Perry, "but we must remember that it was the Almighty that guided us to this victory. The Almighty and the superior American character."

The nearby crew cheered at those words.

"Of course," replied Elliott.

"And yet," continued Perry, his mind beginning to wander back to the immediate situation, "Mr. Edwards," he said to the first officer, "report on the fleeing vessels."

"Aye, sir," Edwards replied with a salute. "The <u>Scorpion</u> has caught up with one of the vessels, the <u>Little Belt</u> we reckon, which has just surrendered. The <u>Trippe</u> will have the <u>Chippewa</u> in no more than a quarter of an hour."

"Very good. Mr. Elliott, do you have any information on why our schooners were unable to enter the fight until so late into the action?"

For just a moment, Alexander saw a flash of embarrassment streak across the captain's face. The junior officer imagined that the captain was replacing the words "our schooners" with "the <u>Niagara</u>" in his head.

"Their…" Elliott stammered. "They were simply unable to capture the wind as effectively as the double masted ships, sir. They could not keep up."

"Well, I'm sure that it was ultimately advantageous that they arrived when they did, and may I congratulate you, Captain, on the well-ordered nature of their attack under your command."

"Thank you, sir."

Perry's half of the exchange was easy and fluid while Elliott seemed to be tripping over his own shoes as he spoke with his commander.

"Very good," said Perry. "I shall return to the <u>Lawrence</u> and receive the British officers there."

"Of course, sir."

"The <u>Niagara</u> is yours, Mr. Elliott."

"Thank you, sir."

The two men saluted each other one more time and parted. Alexander followed along with his brother.

"Commodore…what about…"

"Perhaps later, Mr. Perry," interrupted the commodore. Perhaps he knew that Alexander wanted to hear his feelings on Captain Elliott. "Please retrieve my flag."

Alexander ran to the mainmast, brought down the blue battle flag and, with the help of a nearby seaman, folded it. Tucked neatly under his arm, Alexander carried the flag to the boat which already carried all of the seven Lawrence crewmen who had made the journey as well as Commodore Perry.

"Take your time, Mr. Perry," said the commodore lightly as Alexander jumped the final few rungs of the ladder into the dinghy.

"Sorry, sir…" began Alexander feeling slight embarrassment.

"Never mind, Mr. Perry. Disembark, if you please, Mr. Breese."

While the chaplain pushed away from the Niagara and the crew dipped their worn oars into the lake, cheers erupted from the crew on the deck of the Niagara. The men waved their hats and cheered Perry's name. Captain Elliott was nowhere to be seen.

The commodore remained seated through the return trip. The huzzahs of the American sailors kept him erect in his seat for a time. He tried to politely ignore the cries and "hip-hips" by further inspecting the remains of battle, but he could not hide the smile that subtly crept across his face.

"Look there," whispered Breese from behind Alexander. "They'll never hear our names, but they'll know *his* forever. All the stories of great men you hear, that's them right there, in the flesh."

They were about halfway to the Lawrence when fatigue began to visibly affect the commodore. His straightened back bent as he leaned over. His eyes, which had been open and alert, lost their focus like a man hoping to fall into bed. He propped himself up with a hand on the gunwale. He tried to keep looking up at the smoking hulk that had been his flagship, but the exertions of the day seemed to be finally overwhelming him.

Worried for his brother, Alexander, sitting directly before him, put his hand on Perry's and said, "Oliver" quietly, hoping that no one else could hear him.

"Hello, Alexander," whispered back his brother with a smile. "It almost feels like a dream."

It was at that moment that a distant anthem arose from the distance.

Come, join hand in hand, brave Americans all,
And rouse your bold hearts at fair Liberty's call;
No tyrannous acts shall suppress your just claim,
Or stain with dishonor America's name.

In Freedom we're born and in Freedom we'll live.
Our purses are ready. Steady, friends, steady;
Not as slaves, but as Freemen our money we'll give.

Sung by Augustus on the <u>Lawrence</u>, the tune carried over the gentle waters, creaking wood, and dying crackle of fires. At the beginning of the second verse, Hannibal Collins took up the melody, followed quickly by every seaman in the dinghy. As Alexander joined in, he felt the strength of the words fill him with pride. Between verses he leaned forward to his brother and asked, "Can you hear them, Oliver? Can you hear them singing Liberty's song?"

The commodore's look had changed yet again. Gone were the signs of fatigue, the crooked back, the weary eyes, and the hand on the gunwale. Instead, Commodore Oliver Hazard Perry sat upright with his head held high.

"Yes, I can hear them," he replied softly. "Very good."

Lieutenant Yarnall stood alongside Augustus and Peleg on deck as the returning crew gained the <u>Lawrence</u>'s deck. The acting captain had cleared himself of the down feathers, but his face was still marked with blood that had seeped down from the newly applied bandage around his head. The deck had been half-cleared of the clutter that had accumulated through battle, but the smashed cannons still rested where they had fallen and some of the injured men lay to the side, waiting for help to move below. After a few moments, some seamen came up on deck from the surgery and helped a few of the remaining men to the surgery.

Amidst the mess, Yarnall saluted his returning commanding officer with Augustus, his arm wrapped in a sling, and Peleg who only had half an ear, the other half most likely lost to a musket ball, following suit beside him. Yarnall's face was marked with his typical professionalism, as though the commodore had left the ship to find lunch in town.

"Permission to come aboard, lieutenant?" asked Perry.

"Granted, sir," replied Yarnell cooly.

Perry took a few firm steps to his first officer and grabbed his hand, shaking it firmly with a smile on his face.

"I must apologize, sir," said Yarnall.

"John, what could you possibly have to apologize for?"

"I did not want to strike our colors, sir. Even though we had lost our last gun and I had no one to man any if we even had any left, it still felt like a dishonor to surrender your ship."

"John, you performed admirably. I cannot think of another officer who would have held out longer to greater effect, and I will make sure that America knows it."

Yarnall let a smile crack through his steely exterior for just a moment before returning to his iron-like façade. "Thank you, sir."

Perry slapped Yarnall on the shoulder and nodded in approval. "Now, John. Report?"

The lieutenant paused. His eyes betrayed his grief. "Ah, yes, sir. The count stands at twenty dead and sixty-three wounded, although a few of those might still succumb."

Perry's grin disappeared. In its place, Alexander saw the look of their father when one of his children had hurt themselves, like when Nathaniel had broken his arm falling from a crow's nest back home in Newport.

"Thank you, John," said Perry, dismissing his lieutenant. The two midshipmen began to follow Yarnall, but Perry stopped them.

"Mr. Denham, would you please go to my cabin and find a paper and pencil?"

"Aye, sir."

Peleg turned around and swiftly disappeared below deck

"It's a pleasure to see you well, Mr. Swartwout," Perry said to Augustus.

"Thank you, sir. Doc says that this should heal up nicely," replied the midshipman indicating his bandaged arm.

"Very good. Was that you singing just now?"

"Aye, sir."

"What a wonderful voice."

Augustus smiled from ear to ear. "Thank you, sir."

"Now hop to it. See what help you can be." Perry turned to the seven sailors who had taken the journey to the Niagara with him. "Lend a hand. Get these brave men to Dr. Parsons."

There were only six wounded men left on deck, so the new arrivals split into pairs and took one each. The commodore kept Alexander by his side and walked to the youngest of the injured. He was an ordinary seaman of about eighteen. His shaggy, greasy, and disheveled blond hair nearly covered his face. His eyes stared down at the hastily and amateurishly applied splint tied loosely around his broken leg.

"What's your name?" asked Perry as he knelt down by the sailor.

The young man seemed almost completely unaware of his surroundings for a moment. His head turned from side to side, his eyes scanning the world around him, looking for the distant voice that called out to him. His gaze passed through Alexander without seeing him.

"Sailor?"

At the commodore's second call the seaman found the source of the kindly voice. "Sir," he almost exclaimed as he recognized his commander. He still seemed slow to react. He tried to push himself to his feet but failed as soon as he put any weight on his right leg. He went down with a pitiful cry.

"Stay down," said Perry. "What's your name?"

"Van Dyke, sir. Seaman Van Dyke," he replied after a pause.

"What does your father call you?"

"Charles, sir...Well, actually...Charlie, sir."

"Well, Charlie, Mr. Perry and I are going to help you below deck. I think I can tell whether you can walk or not. Let's see if we can at least get you to your feet."

"Just a moment, sir," said Alexander. He walked around the commodore and began to undo Van Dyke's splint. He used what cloth he could from the original bandage but needed to supplement it with his own bandana which he kept wrapped around his neck. He tied the splint as tightly as possible. With every pull, Van Dyke gasped deeply, but he did not cry out. The job done, Alexander looked up at his patient and seemed to look him attempt a kind smile through the pain to no avail while the sailor's eyes still saw through the midshipman helping him. Oliver only nodded his approval and winked at his little brother.

Peleg regained the deck and sprinted over to Perry, holding an old envelope and a pencil.

"Thank you, Mr. Denham," the commodore said as he scrawled a quick message and handed both the envelope and pencil back to the midshipman. "Take a couple of men and deliver this to General Harrison encamped near Sandusky."

"Aye, sir," replied Peleg as he turned away to follow his orders.

"Very good." Perry said, turning his attention back to Van Dyke. "Now, young man, on your feet."

It was a struggle. The Commodore took Van Dyke's right side and tried to pull the sailor up, but every jostle sapped what little strength he had, sending him crashing back to the deck.

"I'm sorry, sir," said Van Dyke after the second fall.

"It's fine, Charlie. Mr. Perry, I need to use you as leverage."

The two switched sides and Perry pulled Van Dyke up quickly from the sailor's left allowing the sailor to use Alexander as a crutch for his broken right leg. They slowly began to walk across the deck. With each step, Van Dyke pushed all of his weight onto the younger midshipman who was already tired without a broken man sapping the last of his strength, but Alexander offered no complaints. He was eager to help his injured shipmate. He remembered the quiet fortitude that marked his brother's eyes and yearned to replicate it, to feel it, and to be as strong willed as the commodore.

"Tell me, Charlie, how did you hurt your leg?"

"It was..." Van Dyke began before hissing in pain. He seemed to be steadily coming out of his daze. "It was...the enemy...they shot at us...they hit the gun...it swerved to the...to the side...the carriage caught my...my leg...I heard it snap...it snapped when I fell...but, sir...I didn't stop...I fired rifles...I passed gunpowder...I kept fighting...I saw you...you were...you were...they were shooting at you...I couldn't let them..."

Alexander couldn't see the commodore's face, but he did see Perry place his hand on Van Dyke's chest and heard him say, "That was very brave, Charlie. You showed the British what it's like to take on Americans, didn't you?"

"Aye, sir!" the sailor replied. Alexander craned his neck to see the broad smile on the sailor's face. For just that moment, Charles Van Dyke had forgotten all about his pain and his broken leg. He beamed with pride at the conviction his commodore had placed in him.

The crewmen newly returned from the Niagara ascended from the berth deck and went straight to the remaining sailors who were patiently waiting their turn on deck.

"Mr. Collins," said Perry as Hannibal began to pass his commander with a salute. "You haven't lost my flag, have you?"

Hannibal hesitated, quickly glancing down at Alexander who suddenly remembered that he had been the last one with the banner.

"I'm sorry, sir,..." began Hannibal.

"Commodore," interjected Alexander, "I think I left it in the boat, sir."

"Did you?" asked Perry. He looked from his midshipman up to the horizon for a moment. "I must be...Well, it *has* been a very long day, hasn't it?"

"Yes, sir," replied both Hannibal and Alexander in unison.

"Well, never mind who had it last. Could you please retrieve it, Mr. Collins? I'd like to keep the fleet fresh with the memory of a friend, at least," Perry said, referring to Captain Lawrence.

"Aye, sir," said Hannibal who bounded towards the rope ladder and quickly slipped below the taffrail while Perry and Alexander contrived to carry Van Dyke to the doctor.

"When that flag flew on the <u>Niagara</u>, sir, we cheered. Did you hear us, sir?" asked Van Dyke.

"Yes, of course I heard."

"We knew, sir, right then we knew that you'd win the day."

"Remember, Charlie, it was Divine Providence who gave us the favorable wind, and He that brought together such bravery and strength in the American spirit. My contributions were meager additions in comparison to the work of the Almighty."

"I do..." Van Dyke was interrupted when his bad leg dragged along the deck, sending a jolt of pain through his body that even Alexander could feel. When he fought off the agony another time, Van Dyke continued, "I do thank the Almighty, sir, but we all know that we couldn't have won today without you."

Perry smiled down at the sailor. "Thank you, Charlie, but we can't forget your contributions either." The three made a very ginger turn and began to descend the stairs, taking each step singly and carefully. "Your work at the guns...We couldn't have won without you, Charlie."

Van Dyke beamed with pride. "Oh, sir, it could have been any American, sir."

"But it wasn't any American, was it, Charlie? It was you. It takes a certain mettle to do what you did today, and America shall shame itself if it does not celebrate that from this day to its end."

They reached the bottom of the stairs and found help from Dr. Parsons right away who took Perry's load and helped Alexander guide Van Dyke to an open spot on the floor at the back of the crowded surgery. While Alexander rose to his feet, Parsons stayed on his knees to inspect the broken leg and splint.

"That should do for now," said Parsons referencing the bandage as he rose to his feet. "I'll need you to stay there, young man. I'll be back to change your bandages as soon as I can."

"Sir, you won't take the leg, will you?"

"Doesn't look like it, but we'll need to keep an eye on it. You tell me if the skin begins to turn black."

"Aye, sir."

"Parsons?" inquired Perry, directing the surgeon to the most secluded part of the cramped deck with Alexander following close behind.

"How many?" the commodore asked plainly and quietly.

"We just lost one...Hoffman I think his name was, and I don't think that Mays is going to get through the night."

"Mays..." said Perry, trying to remember the name.

"Wilson Mays, sir," said Alexander. "He's the carpenter's mate. The one with the red hair."

"Very good. What happened to him?"

"Shot in the chest by a musket," replied Parsons. "I can't get the ball out, and even if I could, it shattered a couple of ribs and took a bit of his shirt with it. You can already see the signs of infection."

"I want to see him," said Perry.

"Of course, sir, but there's something else you may want to know," replied Parsons.

"What is it?"

"Lieutenant Brooks just passed."

Perry's calm face cracked with bitter sadness. It was only a moment, but the news had brought incredible pain to the commodore.

"He kept asking after you, sir. He inquired about your safety, and the news that we had struck our colors hit him particularly hard. He never even got to hear the news of our victory. When we found out that the Detroit had struck, I came directly to tell the lieutenant, but he was already gone. If only he had lived a few minutes more. If only I had managed to find some way to prolong his life just a bit more...he could have left us with that happy knowledge instead of thoughts of defeat."

"If only he had lived longer? If only you had done more?" asked Perry. "No, Doctor, if only *I* had been faster. Don't blame yourself. That was my failing. If I had only known that a few minutes would have made that kind of difference..." He trailed off, staring at the wooden hull. With a deep breath he said, "Take me to Mays."

And so it was that for over an hour Perry moved from man to man, thanking them for their service and assuring them of their place in history and the accolades they would receive back home. Perry paused by Henry Laub's broken body and prayed silently for a moment. As the Commodore prayed, Alexander looked at his friend's cold corpse and wondered what the young officer was now going to miss. To the man, each injured sailor's spirit lifted as Perry knelt before them, tears forming in his eyes, and embraced them. The commodore was only twenty-seven years old yet some of the men he comforted were nearly twice his age, but they all looked at him as a son lookup up at a caring father.

He was leaving the boatswain's mate James Healan and about to visit the last man he had yet to see when Yarnall came below deck.

"Commodore?" he asked, looking through the mass of bodies.

Perry waved Yarnell over.

"Sir," said Yarnall as he stood over Perry, "the acting captain of the Queen Charlotte has come aboard to officially surrender."

"Very good," replied Perry. "I'll be up in a minute."

"Aye, sir," answered Yarnall, but instead of returning to the deck he lingered as Perry knelt back down before the last sailor.

"What's your name, young man?" he asked the seventeen year old.

"Newport, sir. Newport Hazard."

"Well," replied Perry with a smile on his lips, "quite the curious name you have there. Your father's name was Newport?"

"No sir, my father's last name was Hazard. They gave me my Christian name 'cause of where I was born."

"Your father's name was Hazard and you are from Newport? Well, then we must certainly be cousins. It's curious that I don't know you."

"Begging your pardon, sir, but I thought your name was Perry."

"It is, but my middle name is Hazard, for my grandfather."

"Truly?" asked the sailor as a grin crept across his lips.

"Very much so. Newport, I want you to come to me when we make port. I always want to know more about family, and I want to know how all of my family helped us to defeat the British. Can you do that for me?"

"Aye!" Hazard nearly shouted, but stopped short with a wince of pain.

"Where were you hurt?" asked Perry, holding onto Hazard's arm in support.

"My back, sir. I took two balls to my back. Doc says they're just flesh wounds, but they still hurt."

"You're in the best of hands, Newport." Perry turned and began to walk to the stairs behind Yarnall. After only a few steps, the commodore stopped, put his arm around his brother's shoulders and whispered into his ear, "See if you can make him any more comfortable. Don't do too much, though. He's family by blood, but they're all family now."

"Of course," replied Alexander.

He found Hazard again, knelt by him, and asked, "Can I get you anything, cousin?"

Hazard looked at Alexander funny, his faced scrunched up slightly and his head cocked to one side as he said, "I thought I was the commodore's cousin."

"You are," replied Alexander with an embarrassed smile, "and I'm the commodore's brother."

"You're Mr. Perry, then. I thought you was Mr. Forrest and he was you."

"Nope. I'm Perry."

"So, I have a baby cousin, and I still need to call him 'sir'?" he asked with a smile.

"Looks like it. Do you need anything?"

"I could do with a sip of water."

Alexander pulled out his canteen and handed it to Hazard who took a healthy draught and handed the sack back.

"Where were you in the battle?" asked Alexander as he tried to place Hazard in the crew.

"I was on Mr. Laub's gun crew," he said. The image of Henry's crew came to Alexander as he then recognized the man. "I only felt one of the shots. It was like a bee that digs into ya and won't let go, so I don't know if they both hit at the same time or if I just didn't feel the second of 'em. I tried to stay by my post, but it hurt too much."

"When did you come down?"

"It was about the time that Mr. Swartwout got shot, I think. We came down together."

A whistle sounded the arrival of another British captain on the Lawrence's deck.

"I'm fine, cousin," said Hazard seeing Alexander's desire to find out what was going on.

With his polite clearance to leave, Alexander shook his cousin's hand and walked through the carnage to the stairs and the open air. As he climbed onto the main deck, Alexander closed his eyes and breathed deeply the fresh air. Over the water, smoke, and wood, the young officer could smell a hint of the distant pine trees that surrounded the lake, or was that odor a figment of his imagination? Opening his eyes and looking around he couldn't see any of the nearby shores, all of which hid just beyond the horizon. The sounds of the ship had returned to normal. Forceful but calm orders from Taylor mixed with the gentle lapping of water against the hull and the creak of wood and strain of rope. It was just like many late afternoons Alexander had experienced onboard that ship. Fresh off a round of drilling at the guns, the acrid smell of burnt gunpowder would linger only ever so slightly, the ship lulled into a calm as one watch slowly came to an end and another lazily came into being. But that had been a very different time. That day, Commodore Perry stood proudly on the broken hulk that had once been the USS <u>Lawrence</u> as a British officer offered up his sword.

That young officer couldn't have been much older than Dulaney, who stood next to his commodore. The British officer wore the brevets of a third lieutenant, bowed his head, and held his issue to the victorious commander who refused the weapon with a simple wave of his hand. Alexander was too far away to hear the snippet of conversation between the two, but he was still able to see the enemy officer's stoic face form a small but genuine smile.

After a few moments, the British lieutenant took his leave of Perry's company and joined another British officer who stood along the gunwale. This second officer looked only somewhat older than the one who had just finished speaking with the <u>Lawrence</u>'s commander. He couldn't have been more than twenty, bore the brevets of a second lieutenant, and had a bandage of his right hand, which might have been hiding a missing finger or two. They both looked tired and yet able to stand at attention for another hour without wavering.

The boatswain's mate blew his whistle, signaling another approaching boat, and Alexander walked across the deck to stand next to Dulaney.

"They're just lieutenants?" asked Alexander.

"Would you believe it? They're the most senior officers left on the <u>Queen Charlotte</u> and the <u>Lady Prevost</u>," answered Dulaney in a whisper.

"I heard that General Cornwallis did something like this at Yorktown."

"Except, Mr. Perry," replied Dulaney in a playfully serious tone, "Cornwallis was out of shame. Their captains," the lieutenant indicated the British officers, "are either dead or dying."

"Really?"

"That's what they say. James, the <u>Queen Charlotte</u> man, says Captain Finnis died in the first few minutes of battle. Wilkinson, the lieutenant from the <u>Lady Prevost</u> says that Lieutenant Commander Buchan already lost one leg and may lose an eye as well."

"How horrid," said Alexander as he imagine the injury and suppressed a shiver that ran up his spine.

"Well, it's no worse than we got. Did you hear what happened to Henry? Went below deck after getting shot and got hit by round shot."

"Aye, I heard."

"Don't feel too bad for the British, Alex, we've got our own to mourn."

A moment later, another young British officer climbed aboard the Lawrence's broken deck. This one, another third lieutenant, paused as he steadied himself and made eye contact with the other surrendering officers. There seemed to pass a sense of understanding between them in that fleeting moment. The new lieutenant corrected his posture, pulled down on his disheveled blue uniform to straighten it as much as possible, and gripped his ceremonial sword at his side with pride. As he approached the line of American officers his enemy stood at attention in respect. He marched directly to Commodore Perry, slightly bowed, and held the sword up with both hands.

"Sir," began the British lieutenant, "I present you Commodore Barclay's issue and surrender His Majesty's Detroit."

"Thank you, lieutenant," replied Perry. "Please keep the sword as a sign of good faith."

The lieutenant stood up and brought the weapon to his side.

"What's your name, Lieutenant?"

"Johnson, sir. Avery Johnson, acting second lieutenant."

"A pleasure," replied the commodore. "I am Commodore Oliver Perry."

"Aye, sir. I've heard of you."

"Thank you. May I inquire as to Commodore Barclay's health? I pray nothing has happened to him. I was hoping to perhaps dine with him."

"He would be most honored, I'm sure," replied Lieutenant Johnson. "However, a shot of cannon hit Commodore Barclay in his remaining arm. Our surgeon says that he will lose it."

Perry's face became marked with concern. "How awful. I'll send my surgeon to him as well, as soon as Dr. Parsons is able, to see if there's anything he can do."

"Thank you, sir. I'm sure Commodore Barclay will appreciate any help offered."

"Of course, it is the least that I can do."

Lieutenant Johnson bowed again and joined his fellow officers by the gunwale.

By this point, Alexander was observing all around him like a scientist watching a colony of ants. It was like he was above and outside the events, not a part of them. He couldn't feel his feet beneath him and he wasn't quite sure if he was seeing everything around him with his eyes or if his eyes had closed and the images he saw were from his mind's eye.

"Mr. Perry?" came a voice familiar but strange at the same time. "Mr. Perry? Alex?"

With a sudden effort, Alexander forced his eyes open and saw Dulaney holding his shoulder and looking him straight in the eye. "You seem poorly."

"I'm fine," replied Alexander drowsily. "What's going on?"

"I think you fell asleep."

"No I didn't."

Dulaney ignored Alexander's protestations and called the commodore.

"What is it, Lieutenant?" asked Perry as he joined the pair.

"It's Mr. Perry, sir. I think that he may need to go below."

"Mr. Perry?" asked the commodore of Alexander as he took the midshipman's shoulder in his hand. "How are you feeling?"

Alexander felt a sudden rush of energy that opened his eyes wide. "Great, sir." The energy dissipated as quickly as it had arrived, however, and Alexander felt his eyes steadily close despite his intense efforts.

"I think he should turn in, sir," said Dulaney. "He's just a boy."

"No…" began the commodore, "he's not a boy anymore. Today was a growth spurt. In fact, Alexander looks about a foot taller today than he did yesterday."

The young midshipman found the energy to open his eyes again and see his brother looking at him with respect. Suddenly, keeping his eyes open was no longer a struggle.

"Go below and get some rest, Mr. Perry," said the commodore with a friendly pat on the back.

Alexander wanted to object and stay above, but the setting sun and dimming light was doing nothing but encouraging sleep. "Aye, sir," he replied. Dulaney gave him a playfully subtle shove towards the stairs.

As Alexander descended to the berth deck, he almost ran into a lumbering shadow that turned into Ivan. After a few moments of indiscriminant Russian, the crewman and junior officer found each other in the soft orange glow of a nearby lamp. Alexander, feeling his fatigue creeping over him again, tried to settle with a nod and a salute, but the Russian grabbed the midshipman by the shoulders and began to speak in his native tongue. A moment later, the foreign language dropped away, replaced by broken English. "You," said Ivan, "you are brave. Like captain." Ivan pushed Alexander back, nodded towards the officer's berth and finished with a goodnight in Russian.

Very quickly, Alexander found himself wrapped up in his

hammock. He had no memory of finding the bedding, hanging it up, or if he had greeted anyone else in the berth, but in the moment he finally found himself in the perfect place for sleep, it curiously eluded him. He had nearly fallen into unconsciousness while standing at attention on deck, but in that moment, gently swaying back and forth in the air, he remained awake and almost alert. As he lay there alone in the dark, cursing his stubborn body and mind, Alexander's thoughts began to drift away from his current predicament of sleeplessness. He thought of the flags waving in the breeze. He thought of the clear sapphire sky dotted with distant birds in flight. He remembered the first distant shot, the incomprehensible thunder of cannon, and the eerie quiet afterwards. The memories of anguished screams filled his ears, followed by the cheers of victory, and then the silenced lips of lost friends. And yet, through it all had stood one figure, sounded one voice: that of Commodore Oliver Hazard Perry, his brother. In the midst of battle, and even in the jaws of defeat, his captain had stood tall and resolute. His mere presence had inspired men to take up arms against a superior foe and continue a fight they had no business of winning. The American everyman had sailed, fought, and come out on top of professional sailors sailing under a man who had fought and won alongside Lord Nelson at Trafalgar. Kentucky backwoodsmen had defeated British navy men who had spent more time at sea than on land. Somehow, Alexander felt as though America had come into its own that day: September 10, 1813.

With that thought, Alexander finally felt sleep begin to take over, but the creek of the door interrupted him once again. Just enough to keep him awake, but not enough to jostle him, the creek quickly stopped, replaced by the soft thud of a boot hitting the deck. "Just get in and go get your hammock," he wanted to say expecting one of the midshipmen, but he couldn't find the energy.

"Alex?"

It was Oliver, but Alexander had begun to drift off again, powerless to stop it.

No more words passed his lips. Instead, Oliver Hazard Perry stood there quietly as Alexander finally found sleep and drifted off into unconsciousness.

THE END

Dear General:

We have met the enemy and they are ours. Two ships, two brigs, one schooner and one sloop.

Yours with great respect and esteem,
O.H. Perry

Bibliography

A Citizen of New York. (1835). *A Biographical Notice of Com. Jesse D. Elliott.* Philadelphia.

Bancroft, G. (1891). *History of the Battle of Lake Erie.* New York: Robert Bonner's Sons.

Bellin, J. N. (n.d.). *Partie Occidentale de la Nouvelle France ou du Canada.* London.

Birch, T. (n.d.). *Perry's Victory on Lake Erie.* Pennsylvania Academy of the Fine Arts, Philadelphia.

Brant, I. (1961). *James Madison Commander in Chief.* New York: The Bobbs-Merril Company.

Calvert, G. (1854). *The Battle of Lake Erie.* Providence: B.T. Albro.

Capt. W.W. Dobbins. (1913). *History of the Battle of Lake Erie.* Erie: Ashby Printing.

Hickey, D. R. (2012). *The War of 1812: A Forgotten Conflict, Bicentennial Edition.* Chicago: University of Illinois Press.

Mackenzie, A. S. (1843). *The Life of Commodore Oliver Hazard Perry.* New York: Harper & Brothers.

Niles, J. M. (1820). *The Life of Oliver Hazard Perry.* Hartford: R. Storrs.

Parsons, U. (1862). *Brief Sketches of the Officers Who Were in the Battle of Lake Erie.* Albany: J. Munsell.

Patterson, C. R., & French, H. B. (n.d.). *Battle of Lake Erie, 10 September 1813.* U.S. Naval Academy, New York City.

Roosevelt, T. (1882). *The Naval War of 1812.* New York: G.P. Putnam's Sons.

Stuart, G. (n.d.). Portrait of Oliver Hazard Perry. *Portrait by Gilbert Stuart.* Boston.

The Newport Historical Society. (1913). *Items of Interest Concerning Oliver Hazard Perry in Newport.* Newport: Mercury Publishing.

Whitcombe, T. (n.d.). *Bataille des Saintes, 12 avril 1782.* London.

Woodworth, L. (n.d.). The Brig Niagara under full sail, off of South Bass Island, Ohio on Lake Erie. *Brig Niagra full sail.*

About the Author

David Vining lives in Charleston, SC with his wife and son. In addition to writing, he is also an avid movie fan and loves watching the Oakland Athletics.

His favorite drink is Scotch, in case you ever meet him and want to every immediately get on his good side by providing him with a nice dram (with only a dash of water, please).

Other Works by David Vining

Short Story Collections:
A Light in the Darkness
A Boy and His Satellite
Mutiny!
Old Magic in a New World
Shoes for Two Soldier Sons

Made in the USA
Monee, IL
29 July 2023

40104583R00062